Dark Waves and Light Matter

Dark Waves

The University of Georgia Press   *Athens & London*

and Light Matter

ESSAYS BY ALBERT GOLDBARTH

Published by the University of Georgia Press
Athens, Georgia 30602
© 1999 by Albert Goldbarth
All rights reserved
Designed by Erin Kirk New
Set in 10 on 14 Sabon by G & S Typesetters, Inc.
Printed and bound by Maple-Vail Book Group
The paper in this book meets the guidelines for
permanence and durability of the Committee on
Production Guidelines for Book Longevity of the
Council on Library Resources.

Printed in the United States of America

03 02 01 00 99   C   5 4 3 2 1

Library of Congress Cataloging in Publication Data

Goldbarth, Albert.
Dark waves and light matter : essays /
by Albert Goldbarth.
p.   cm.
ISBN 0-8203-2126-5 (alk. paper)
I. Title.
PS3557.O354D37   1999
814'.54—dc21   98-55457

British Library Cataloging in Publication Data available

for Nathan

a book for the book man

Dos gan-eydn un dem gehenem ken men hobn oyf der velt.

Heaven and hell can be had in this world.

 —Yiddish proverb

ACKNOWLEDGMENTS

Square of Light: *Parnassus* (reprinted in *The Best American Movie Writing 1998*)

A History: *The Iowa Review*

The Whole of a Person's Nature: *The American Literary Review*

My Week Aboard a UFO!!!: *Ploughshares*

Keepers of the Flame: *The Iowa Review*

Whitman's America: *The Seneca Review*

To Write of Repeated Patterns: *The Iowa Review* (reprinted in *The Pushcart Prize XVIII: The Best of the Small Presses,* and in *Hard Choices: An Iowa Review Reader*)

The Lake: *The Georgia Review* (reprinted in *Harper's* and listed in "Notable Essays," in *The Best American Essays 1997*)

The Lemmix: *Tolstoy's Dictaphone: Technology and the Muse* (Graywolf Press)

Both Definitions of *Save: The Iowa Review*

I'd also like to acknowledge the good company of good people in a bad place: Kim Hamilton, Don Wineke, Lisa Moser, Rita Costello, Kathleen Davis, Kevin Colgan, Robert Flinn, Cole Rachel. And of course Skyler.

CONTENTS

Dark Waves and Light Matter

Square of Light

"But sir, my name is on a list . . ."

"You think you're special then? You're a lump. You're one more formless lump."

"The mayor's office they signed the list, sir . . ."

"Mayor my ass. Four hours, not one minute more. You won't get paid here for those four hours, do you understand?"

"The list . . ."

"Do you understand?"

She does. She goes, she leaves the gates of Pryor's Manufactory Cottons with the note in her carpetbag purse. She is a formless lump. Her father is a formless lump, her mother is a formless lump, and seven siblings share two beds like pallid balls of dough that still await a baker's shaping touch.

I don't think we can be ourselves again—I mean our original selves, before the twentieth-century silver-screen-TV-and-magazine-ad-infonet-athon provided its thousands of models for any possible emoting.

You were on the bed, your arm raised in an eloquent, skewed L that meant dismissiveness, but meant it in the language of an image of a gesture of dismissiveness picked up from this or that iconic figure which preceded us.

And I could almost envy, a moment, the neighborhood's singular mutter-and-spit old man we find on benches in the summer swatting demons off, his mumbles and his raw gesticulation un-provided-for by anything—so, pure in a way; a shape outside ideas of succession.

I could see your mind's eye calling forth its stored range of ce-lebrity dismissiveness, in microseconds, selecting a posture from out of similar second-bests . . . In an artist's sketchbook once, I saw the body of a woman with her left arm lifted, only it was dozens of rehearsal left arms lifted, she was waving like a hydra on the smudgy page.

It's this way: say a woman wants to rent a cast-of-suntanned-thousands Biblical Epic video, something with sandals and shields and plumes and golden chariots and a love scene near a pyramid as the sky storms. And a man prefers to rent the story of four *echt*-pensive people at a table, talking, talking.

Then the mode of what they're arguing about instructs the ar-guing itself. The hothouse thespian hauteur of Nefertiti; and the generated chill from a man who has studied shoestring-budget portrayals of *auteur* emotional freon.

"You will simply climb one side of the ladder until you reach its top, at a natural speed, don't hurry, and then at the top pose—*so,*" and Eadward Muybridge, in his graying frowzled garden-of-a-beard and eternally-on-him-whether-out-of-doors-or-in black crumpled Amish-look surveyor's hat, swings one leg grandly in back of himself, and lifts his arms and puffed-up chest aspiringly upward, with the full effect of a ballerina's kick *cum* Viking dragon prow, "and count to five, and then simply climb back down. Do you see?"

"And I will be undressed?"

"And you will be undressed."

There's silence now in this building on the well-trimmed Penn-sylvania University grounds. He fancies he can hear the light in its ceaseless lap against the outside walls—*his* light, his wrought gold that he captures and condenses like an alchemist in an alembic.

"Elsie—" What to say? She's new. A friend of the provost's daughter. She's the only model who's shown so far today, and the cameras he'd swear are lowly purring in impatience to be used.

He nods at one of them now, his lovely four-foot box with its thirteen Dallmeyer lenses. "I will be here with the camera, Elsie, fully forty-nine feet away from the ladder."

If this reassures her, there's no visible sign. She *knows* this is "important," that it's "Art" or "Science" or some such term come down to touch her life from where it's been carved on a marble entablature, and yet . . . and yet . . . What tale will she tell them, when she returns to her day at the folding-line of Pryor's Manu-factory Cottons?

"Dozens have preceded you, Elsie, women, men, all—" He has an idea. "*This,*" and he unties the leather cover of an album and removes two sheets of developed images, "*this* will either send you fleeing in horror, or convince you of the . . . *naturalness* with which we view the project."

One is eighteen sequenced shots of *Athlete swinging a pick,* and one is forty-four of *Model No. 95, ex-athlete, aged about sixty, ascending and descending incline,* and bearing a fifty-pound weight in twenty-two of these snaps. The man is naked. The man is Muybridge, chuckling now over his sixty-two tiny selves.

"You see?"

"But Mr. Muybridge," she says—is there a nascent twinkle in her eye?—"when you was a-posin' for these . . . ?"

"Yes, Elsie?"

". . . sir, *I* wasn't behind the camera." And then the both of them, chuckling. She milks the joke of her sly observation. "*I* never made no such photographs."

"Elsie . . ." He fully undoes the album, and then two more,

and fans a hundred sheets across the table, selecting some, pointing in rapid succession at his astonishing serial studies, naked men at cricket, boxing, fencing, horseback riding, naked women running, somersaulting, rolling hoops with sticks, a trotting camel on loan from the Pennsylvania Zoo, a greyhound, a milk-white parrot in flight, more naked men (one pugilist feigns a knockout), a deer, a woman performing jumping jacks, and all of them immediately blinking out of themselves and into their next selves . . .

". . . nobody, *nobody,* has ever made such photographs."

If you run beside an ancient Egyptian temple mural, skimming your vision linearly along those beaked and snouted anthrobodied gods, and the captives taken in war, and the stately parade of geese at the Nile's shore . . .

Does it "move?"

It's "motion" "pictures."

Yes, or if you take a vase, a cayenne-red Greek vase with its circular frieze of courtesans or wrestlers in flat black profile, if you spin it, if you place it back on its potter's wheel and spin it . . .

"For Claude Monet, there are 100,000 images," art historian Elie Fraue declares, "in the space of a second." How to separate them, into single painted moments that maintain their continuity? It's 1891: Monet is painting "frames" of what could be a continuous "reel" of haystacks ageing over—*ageing into*—time . . .

But let's go back to May 4, 1880. Eadward Muybridge tonight is lecturing at the San Francisco Art Association Rooms; he's introducing his quaint invention by which his sequenced photographs of a horse in motion are set around the circumference of a glass disc and projected by a lantern onto a screen, while a handle is turned and the disc is rotated.

Kevin MacDonnell: "To Muybridge belongs the honor" (not that it isn't debated) "of inventing the movie."

In 1888, on a lecture tour that brings him to Orange, New Jersey, Muybridge meets Thomas Alva Edison, who received a demonstration of the "zoopraxiscope," and who "purchased a set of Muybridge's horse pictures. When he invented his revolutionary cine-camera, using the long perforated films we know today, he is said to have made his first movie by copying these photographs." By 1910 the Edison Company's already publishing *Edison Kinetogram,* announcing "Edison Films to Be Released," including *Frankenstein.*

Imagine for your first time seeing the battle of love and monstrousness in a form that subsumes you entirely. It's said that people continued to sit there, demanding not the movie again, but just the square of light itself—as if even that were instructive.

This isn't an easy confession to make, but I'm the kind of guy who leaves at the end of a Jerry Lewis movie duplicating Jerry Lewis's wacky ham abrasiveness for a day—it gets inside me, like a hand inside a puppet. I'm suddenly honking the noses of friends. James Dean: that bee-stung sneer. James Bond (the Sean Connery Bond): that killer *haute monde* eyebrow-arch.

Weightlifter Gordon Scott was the Tarzan of my childhood (*Tarzan's Hidden Jungle* appeared in 1955; Scott stayed with the role through 1960): rugged good looks, a touch more pretty than craggy. Forty years go by, I'll still startle up from the work at hand (a poem; or the drone of committee work; or the fussy upkeeps houses require, and love) and I'll have the half-subliminal flash of that immense heart-whanging parabolic sweep-through-air on a jungle vine: a single green and graceful scallop.

It's this way: fifty years before that day when Muybridge redefined the gallop of the horse for us (*renumerated* it, actually, with photographic proof that all four hooves are off the ground at once, a refutation of centuries of equestrian depiction in the fine arts), sheets of plate glass came to the streetside windows of snooty shops in Regent Street and Oxford Street; some, nine feet tall by five wide. Now the idea of "display," of spacious, elegant interiors. And now the idea of shop assistants selected for certain paradigms of physical appeal. With all-night lighting installed, pedestrians would gather in enormous knots before these windows, learning what they wanted to become.

Today, when the tonier big-bucks fashion models strut their ramps in versions of otherdimensional-sci-fi-funk-punk-faery-fireman-shepherdess-hookerapparel, it's harder to remember, but these *are* "models"—these are paragonic structures—and their trickle-down will fill our common psychic air, will determine the mall-talk of Omaha. The most stellar of these, of course, will even try "making it" in the movies.

We think of Hollywood as "the land of dreams": it's one of Hollywood's favorite self-descriptions. But the reverse is true. The movies *are* our lives—writ large. And if they're often wish-lives, if they're nothing but otherdimensional fashion . . . still, our minds try on those giants' clothes, those clothes consisting of shadow and light, and for better or worse we wear them into one another's days and nights.

The ancient High Myths, with their cycles of gods and hellspawn, have deserted us (or we, them). Religion is a thin shell, not an infrastructure. And yet we hunger for precepts, modes of conduct and social assurance ("The name is Bond . . ." *pause-pause* then turn and give her a javelin stare full-tilt, oh fourteen-year-old manboy lost in the wilds ". . . James Bond"). We *need* a world larger than we are. No—we need a world larger than we are *that addresses* what we are.

I have to ask now: did I love my father? Irving Goldbarth, weary, decent, family-minded peddler of Metropolitan Life Insurance through the penny-ante living rooms of Cicero, Illinois, at

10 P.M., who never lied to me, not once, whose voice in the blessing over the Hanukkah candles wavered like the flames, who danced in his underwear in the kitchen (*"hoochiekoochiekoo"*), who embarrassed me (he'd never read a book), who worked the weekends so that *I* could lead a life of reading books, who walked the dog and waited patiently for it to pee on its signature trash can, even in winter, even when Dr. Steinitz said that in winter he'd have to wear the breathing mask, for his heart . . . did I love him? Yes. Did I learn the rudiments of what it is to walk this planet from him? Yes.

But I wouldn't have spent ten minutes trying to emulate my father. I could be Tarzan or Bond in my head for a month.

She's placed a thumb in each of her ears and spread her fingers apart, like wiggling, cockamamie antlers.

"See? Like this? And I can spin around like a toy top." Both of them giggling—she and Muybridge.

"Or so?" She pulls her mouth grotesquely wide, then squats and hops like a frog—assured her audience will be won, assured by her eighth time back to pose for Art and Science that she can clown this way and still retain the composure of a professional conspiring in hijinks with a coworker. This is the ambience he's created for her, and she's risen from out of some beat-down, bottom shapelessness to make herself over, into the image this newfound world has seeded for her and that she's continued to lavishly nurture.

"Or simpler, sir?" She pairs her hands beneath her chin, as if for prayer, and bows elegantly from the waist, in slow repeated clockwork fashion.

"Elsie, Elsie. You're as frisky today as a pent-up cat. *Relax.* I need to bring more lenses over, from the shed outside. When I return, we'll think of some proper posing." They both laugh: *proper!* The day before she spent her four-hour session juggling a pear and an orange, then climbing the ladder with a circus parasol held in either hand.

He leaves her standing before the project's standard backdrop, a floor-to-ceiling grid of two-inch squares created of taut white cord against black. He lingers amid a pile of Carbutt's Keystone Dry Plates, checking the shipment. When he returns . . . She's cut a cat—*a pent-up cat*—from a roll of butcher paper, and set it clawing its way up the grid.

She's inventive that way, and she notices he's appreciative of her gamin creativity, and this inspires more. She milks her jokes. Just to see what will happen, he thinks up another excuse for leaving the hall. It's a game now: he returns to find she's papered the exes and ohs of tic-tac-toe into nine of the squares.

"Enough. Here's a pan and some sawdust. Go, pretend that you're feeding the chickens."

It *is* enough—perhaps too much. The truth is, they've created an Elsie so aware of her bearing (after all, these are supposedly photos of people caught in common, candid motion) that her modeling sessions are some of the least productive. While her "Elsieness" strengthens in charm and durability, it translates into something artificial on the proof sheets. Anyway, the project is nearly over. He likes her, they all like her, he could see her on his arm, with a foamed-over pail of beer and a platter of iced raw oysters . . . hmmm . . . Regretfully, though, they ease her out of the schedule. Her note is not renewed.

And from then on . . . ? Muybridge in Paris, Muybridge in London, Muybridge addressing the gathered grandees of the worlds of Art and Science, Muybridge opening Zoopraxographical Hall at the World's Columbian Exposition in Chicago (1893). "On 8 May 1904 he died and was cremated in Woking."

No, I mean Elsie. Back to the folding-line. Back to the twelve-hour days of spirit-vitiating labor. Although there's this:

"You! Havercomb! Elsie Havercomb! Step from the line!"—a

loutish assistant manager. "Production rate for your section is down, and I swear that if you don't—"

Something about the set of her jaw, the unexpected aliveness in her eyes now. Lamely, letting it dwindle: "Havercomb, just get back to the line." And she turns from him like royalty.

The same year that the most fashionable of plate glass windows opened up its opulent realm of furs and buttery leather goods on Regent Street, and started its work commercially mentoring people into gaining newly elevated concepts of themselves . . . that same year, a Dr. Horn from Salzburg reports that there, in the infirmary, was "a girl of twenty-two years of age . . . who had been brought up in a hog-sty among the hogs, and who had sat there for many years with her legs crossed. She grunted like a hog, and her gestures were brutishly revolting."

The annals are filled with the various mewlings of humans-raised-by-animals stories, from (the first of contemporary record) the wolf-boy of Hesse, who was found in the woods in 1341 "and growled, and beshat himself naked in public, and raw meat only would he eat; and this while on his knees," through (for example from 1971, in the *London Daily Mirror*) the gazelle-boy of the Spanish Sahara near Río de Oro, seen leaping with the herd. The anthropologist Jean-Claude Armen watched the gazelle-boy "approach gazelles and lick their foreheads in a sign of recognition."

The monkey-boy of northern Ceylon (1973, in the *London Sunday Times*) "is speechless, grunts in a half-wolf, half-goat way, and bites and claws at anyone who shows him affection." The bear-girl of Fraumark was found in a den, a woman/girl of about eighteen, asleep on a floor of bear scat: "She refused to eat anything but raw meat, roots and the barks of trees."

Those for whom Another Kind is precedential.

So much of us, inside us, is innate. As for the rest . . . Somebody hypnotized at that furrier's gold-and-ruby-highlighted, easeful, splendid family of mannequins: a schematic display of not only adornment, but of the rules of a possible life.

And somebody (just as "happy"? how are we to judge?) on her rump in a mire of pigness.

How could she have been otherwise, without a god or a guide or a single scene from *Casablanca*? Without, essentially, a window: into the world of what and how to be.

✦

"Heroes? *Heroes?*" asks one of the likeably nasty midget-rapscallions in the classic camp-adventure flick *Time Bandits,* almost spitting the words. "What do *they* know about a day's work?"

And it's true. For example:

The sun in Sumeria savages the everyday afternoon air, as you'd expect. As you'd expect, sun makes a burning mote in the center of every sweatbead. Gilgamesh cuts down a tree. Gilgamesh, whose father was a *lillu*-demon, King of Uruk who founded civilization in the Seven Cities, fells a great *huluppu* tree with a dragon's nest at its base and the terrible *Zu*-bird in its crown "and in its midst the demoness Lilith had built her dwelling."

I wouldn't say he doesn't strain. I'd say he doesn't sweat. Exertion is never that intimate for him. I've looked at the cylinder seals, I've read the cracked, translated tablets, and the sweat isn't there, no, not at the lip of the Well of Immortal Life, not in the wrestle-pit of lions or by Humbaba's mountain, and not at the tree, and not at the one great swing or at the one clean bite it requires.

But look at flipped-through pages from *The American Photographic Postcard, 1900–1920:*

Here above the mill at Loleta "Mr. Gibson is the 3rd from left and Harris our son is the 4th from right"—nine men are ready to pole a background of hundreds of ton-jumbled fifteen-foot logs. It always looks like fifty men's work, a hundred. There are always nine. I come back often, and count—there are nine, their heavy faces say their easy poses have nothing to do with their work, which is hard, too long, and depleting; and the small empty corner up in the right says: air has been converted today, into just a new place to hold wood.

And the light in the simple sky and the cumbersome cameras of 1910 are saying, flash by flash, and ice delivery truck by hod by plow by shovel, that twelve men in Ohio are halfway up a frame for "Duncan, the Round Barn Man." I close the book. Days later I open it. Yes: there's still halfway to go. They wake up every morning and know it, and there are overalls here so rumpled, they carry permanent shadows in places no matter where the sun or how strong.

I won't suggest that Hercules was ignorant of effort, in the stables, "diverting the course of a river" to cleanse their waist-high filth. But on the white-ground jar and the red-figured platter, the sun pours down in a column behind him, a clement and almost sculptural sun. He doesn't pant. The stables are newly fresh, and here he is now, busy posing as if for a calendar featuring surfer boys. Later there will be bonfire feasts, a speech, a green wreath, and some nubile dancers.

And later there will be, and there will always be, "Mrs. Adeline Havercomb Maggody and sister, Mrs. Elsie Havercomb Atkins. During their 35 years of service at Pryor's Manufactory Cottons *Pennsylvania's Very Finest* they have boxed and folded 71,280,000 sheets of Pryor's excellent products." (Elsie's the one with the elfin cockiness.)

Seventy-one-million, two-hundred-eighty-thousand.

Smile. Hold it. (flash)

Seventy - one - million, two - hundred - eighty - thousand - and - one . . .

✳

*Perhaps you have seen me. I know well, my purpose was merely
that of a symbol, "equals," "times," or that of the person drawn
as a code, with sticks for limbs and a circle for a head. I could be
anyone. I was* specifically asked *to be anyone. I do know what a
"portrait" is; and mine are not. I could have been the woman on
her toe-tips just as readily, or the woman lifting imaginary laun-
dry from a real tub. I could have been a man fencing the air, or a
bicyclist. I was, we all were, series of connected dots upon the
graph we posed against. Our flesh it was, that connected the dots,
our own insistent flesh; but what it said, for all that, was identity-
less: a kind of live geometry.*

*And yet when I look at myself here thirty-five years back, I
take my individual pleasure; this, I think, was the moment I first
understood that a pleasure* could *be an autonomy, that I was
something more than a human unit inside a human machine.
You see?—here?—these are the sturdy, wheaten haunches that
Tallow, the manager, couldn't bring to his bed like trophies although he threatened dire consequences every week for a decade
until the shearing engine one day went off track and ate him up
to the waist; and these are the sassy breasts that brought the
haughty Lemuel Atkins to his knees; and here, your finger can
trace the strength of this back, that never gave out, and sup-
ported—once Father had disappeared into too many brandy-
wine cordials—a mother and six unappreciative ne'er-do-well
brothers and sisters, bless them anyway each one (excepting
Henry perhaps, the rotter).*

*You see?—in this one, here, I smile, and Lemuel won't be
thrown from the spook-eyed strawberry roan for another twenty
years. Time stops here. Nothing can take away this smile.*

*I patterned myself, for the rest of my days, on the form you see
here making itself completely in eight four-hour modeling sessions. I never regretted it.*

And these are the ones in which I posed with Isabella, my friend, the contact who recommended me to the mayor's offices in the first place. Here—the badminton ones, and the sillier ones with the pillow fight. Perhaps you have seen the ones in which she splashes me with a pail of water, its contents entirely flung in the air and caught there forever uncurling like a fern; or like the silvery train to a gown at my coronation.

:✦:

Nobody really argues over which video to rent. They argue over lassitude-versus-retentiveness, they argue over God and no-God, immediate-gratification-or-future-security, they argue over money, over seemliness. The video is only the mask for this, the key, the lever.

Soon, they compromise: they watch the video *she* wants. But she has to feel indebted for a while.

They watch it—something alternately steamy and deific, about a slave girl's rise to queenship through the (overgilded, technicolor) pharaonic bed—they watch it sleepily and chatter, easy and sweet but with a small glint of the squabble's after-edge, and when it's over and rewound they chatter sweet-and-squabbly more, until his sentences grow scratchy and distracted, yes and her attention warbles like a song on the whipping tip of a thread-thin wavelength on the radio when the car speeds ever out of range, it's here now, what's she thinking, reed in a slipstream, now it's gone . . .

She walks outside . . .

the night sky feels as snug as a head-dress—in a way; and in a way she's aware of its limitlessness, its dizzying outward-onward. She's been given—since the royal eye has declared her a sexual favorite—a break this evening from her line-work in the stuffy deeps of the House of Folding the Sacred Cloth. It's fold-and-fold-and-pile-it, and fold-and-fold-and-pile-it, and the gossip of Takh-te and Natra-tiy beginning to harden like plugs of glue in her ears . . .

Out here, away from them, and away from the lusty touch of He-Who-Is-the-Shining-Lotus-of-the-Two-Lands, she can be a whole number again—before the duties all resume, and so refraction her—can be a number feeling that it might rise to a higher power.

A laggard breeze from off the river reaches her skin . . . The cries of the compound's geese . . . She looks up at the sky, at its fiery diagram of connection-points—the Nurturers and Warriors and Devils and Martyrs and Shapers who have always burned up there no matter who we were down here, and always will. We *are* those elements—in mortal combination. She flexes her nostrils. If she had a wish . . . So simple:

She wants to be like the stars.

A History

There were some they called "The Butcher" or "Sawhandle." He was more scientific than that, more . . . delicate really; he had a lightsome touch and could arrange his elaborate patterns of electrodes like a florist finicking over each leaf of a lavish piano-top display. In fact he often thought of the wires as stems, and of the screams they'd occasion as flowers—as flowers as huge as the jaws of dogs prised open by agony—blossoming punctually in the air of the makeshift experiment room. The finer equipment he'd requisitioned had yet to be approved by Berlin; because the switch he needed to throw was as big as a good-sized rat trap, that's the sobriquet they gave him, "Doctor Switches." He knew it. He wore the name with pride.

Once, on a social call to a similar camp, its supervising interrogation officer had invited him to a session. Evidently its power, its raw sense of invention, was supposed to impress him. Instead he was appalled by the way the energy he channeled with such consummate precision—the lovely voltage—was used so clumsily here. A Jew-slut had been tied by wrists and ankles to the corners of an improvised examination table; from the sloshing murk of a bucket, a nurse-attendant in an immaculate lab coat and mud-encrusted gardening gloves had lifted an electric eel and then, on orders, using both hands and grunting as if working a heavy shovel, had doubled it up inside the patient's filthy cunt.

"If you wait, you can see its startling effect on a man, a rectal insertion."

But he was eager only for returning home to his hugely more aesthetic and intellectual explorations. Not uncommonly, he'd play a recording of Chopin in the background and, with the switch at use like a maestro's baton, he'd have his patients jerkily dance in rhythm to the musics.

✦

The rubber monsters of '40s and '50s "horror movies" aren't very frightening—one looks something like a twenty-story burlap bag of turnips, one is nothing more than a flapjack, if a flapjack flew, if a flapjack were the size of a downtown parking lot and flew, and dangled ducklike webs from its belly.

But what they *stand for,* the irrepressible hungers of furred, werewolfian beasts and formally-caped, vampiric coquettes and grandees . . . these are incipient in us, and their rising in the night, on the screen, calls forth from us a rise of psychic gooseflesh. What are all of those behemoth-things unleashed by undersea atomic tests—the populous dynasty of Godzilla, smashers of skylines into rubble and dust—if not the reproachful ghosts of Hiroshima walking the land?

The (filmic) Frankenstein mythos, in its own cartoony way, repeatedly plays against the World Wars.

For example: in *Son of Frankenstein* (1939), we're introduced to "the crisply authoritarian (Police Inspector) Krogh," defined by "both a monocle and a wooden arm to hold it. . . . When he swivels his arm up with an audible screech, viewers in 1939 couldn't help but be reminded of the hordes of German soldiers and civilians giving the mindless, stiff-armed Nazi salute." Krogh is played to the military hilt by Lionel Atwill, who dons an identical role in three succeeding films of the corpus, through 1945.

Even as early as 1935, in director James Whale's brilliant German Expressionist–tilted sets for *The Bride of Frankenstein,* the characters enact a prescient foreboding. The movie "has a feel-ing about it of helplessness before a future that was becoming clearer and more terrifying all the time. Mussolini, already in power for many years, was about to invade Ethiopia; Hitler, whose New Order was two years old in 1935, was giving life to a huge disciplined war machine and preaching the myth of Aryan superiority."

Enter Dr. Pretorious, "the maddest of all mad scientists" (clearly necrophile, alchemist and inveigling dictator-wannabe), who grows the artificial brain that Henry Frankenstein neatly sews into the Bride. The dream of Pretorious is a worldscale ap-plication of the make-your-skin-crawl science he's perfected al-ready, and from his largeish samples case displays for Dr. Frank-enstein: sealed glass jars of lab-created homunculus-sized people —in one a mermaid, in one a bishop in robes and miter, in one a pivoting ballerina. "The science is eugenics. Contemporary Nazi mythology promised a race of men like gods, created through se-lective breeding and elimination of the defective and inferior. . . . Pretorious is a perfect parody of a . . . Hitler."

The sheeted and as-yet-unliving body of the Bride is made available to the generating power of an electrical storm; shots of lightning raggedly blast the screen; then: "She's alive! ALIVE!" Perhaps her origin serves as explanation of the silver zigzag bolts that streak up either side of her frizzled, extravagant Nefertiti 'do.

This is the same enlivening spark that, four years earlier, in 1931, zaps Boris Karloff into his stumbling, touching, monsterly· life—as Whale's script ostentatiously calls it, "the great ray that first brought life into the world."

The capture of natural forces for this artificial life "suggests . . . the Promethean travesty of cosmic power put in mortal hands." "Now I know what it feels like to *be* God!" Henry Frankenstein exults.

James Whale understood well the consequences of vast means worked relentlessly toward small-minded ends. He was British,

and served in World War I, and spent time—hellish time—
interred in a German prisoner-of-war camp.

.✦.

Electricity.

The first of all film *Frankenstein*s (in 1910) was produced by
the Edison Company.

In May of 1957—electroshock at a psychiatric hospital having
left him "in agony day and night," as his final note expressed it—
James Whale, who couldn't swim, walked out to the pool he'd
had installed for friends and dove aggressively into it, striking his
head on the bottom of the shallow end, blanking out, drowning.

.✦.

> Some say they were used in the laboratory because they were about to
> be used in the preparation of the soup.
> —Asimov's *Biographical Encyclopedia of Science and Technology*

And now with the study, and now with the passion, of someone
fashioning earrings for a lover—for his lover's lobes, her perfect,
flickable, nibble-me lobes, as fleshy as her bulbous middle toe,
and as tart with a day's sebaceous coating . . . *careful . . . easy . . .*

Pairs of severed frogs' legs, set on brass hooks. These he's attached to the iron lattice surrounding the hanging garden of his
house. O quite a sight, in Bologna, in 1787 . . . *there! . . .*

Now less the lover, and more the fretful general inspecting his
troops. Is everything regimental? The sky is a darkening dough.
The wind is bringing weather that cracks like carriage whips . . .
soon . . . The man is impatiently pacing oblongs in front of his
unlikely experiment . . . *now!*

A thunder to rattle your earbones, a thunder to quiver the very
snot in your head like aspic—and a lightningstorm to match.
And yes . . . and yes . . . they twitch like live things on the rail-

ing!—and he roars at them, a drunken harem dancing-master in front of this nightmare chorus line.

Galvani /galvanic, galvanized, galvanometer/ at work on the theory of "animal electricity."

They had a saying then, about something that finally turns out valuable, when it might have just as readily gone unrecognized and been thrown out: *And to think that it was saved from the soup.*

Did it storm, that famous summer night in 1816—Byron's villa at Lake Leman, with the snaggled line of the Swiss Alps in the distance? Did the sky unloose its angers?

In the movie it does. A pseudohistorical "prologue" to *The Bride of Frankenstein* brings us Byron, Shelley, and Mary Wollstonecraft Godwin Shelley herself (as played by Elsa Lanchester—also "the Bride"), in stagey, rapt discussion of the philosophical implications of monsterdom and its creation. Mary's set her embroidery hoop aside, to join the talk. They're grouped (with four enormous Russian wolfhounds) around a baronial fireplace appropriate to our sense of gothichistorico pomp. And outside—also moodily appropriate—the sky, like a great black carpet, is beat by great electrical gouts of celestial energy.

In "real life"? . . . It rained, that's all she tells us from across the years, "it proved a wet, ungenial summer and incessant rain often confined us for days to the house." But whether that night the rain was rumbled and gashed, or simply a bland uninterrupted inconveniencing, we don't know.

We can picture, though, our nineteen-year-old author-about-to-be, with telling empathy—can see the growing frown of concentration "v" the flesh between her eyes; can see her turn from, then accept, those buried and intimate fears of her own that start to feed her public fiction; even see her (she's been left alone at Villa Diodati while her male compatriots traipse the Alps for a few days) startle at everyday creaks, and doublecheck the staggered weave of shadows of trees at the window.

And we know the stories she'd have heard, the way today in the 1990s we'd hear the party chatterers wonder casually at genetic cloning, "virtual reality," the algae farming of Mars. She tells us Byron and Shelley "talked . . . of Dr. Darwin . . . who preserved a piece of vermicelli in a glass case, till by some extraordinary means it began to move with voluntary motion."

Shelley, her angeldevil lover with hair like mussed wings. He'd experimented himself, with fuming sulfur and rigged-up battery apparatus. He thought we might reshape the *given* of human life in more beneficent, enabling ways, that science would free us from centuries of tyranny. He dabbled and dreamed.

Yes, and if vermicelli—"Perhaps a corpse would be reanimated." Why not? "Galvanism had given token of such things."

He'd experimented himself, with fuming sulfur and rigged-up battery apparatus. He thought we might reshape the *given* of human life in more beneficent, enabling ways, that science would free us from centuries of tyranny. He dabbled and dreamed. It was, after all, the great age of the amateur discoverer.

"Specialization" by "discipline" didn't exist; the juicy, extant informations were available and, beyond that, *comprehensible,* to whoever could read. Young clerics and court clerks stalked across chalk quarries with an archeologist's scatter of gougers and scrapers in their wicker baskets. A tanner was a chemist, or a miner a hydraulicist; a painter—an "artist"—seriously advanced the "science" of optics. For the first time, women entered these grand pursuits. The poor, if they were shrewd, could keep their eyes wide, and learn, and apply what they learned, and make their contribution, and advance. The horizon was unrestricted. Its wind went *whoosh:* the sound of the times. Their sign: a winged test tube.

For example, Humphry Davy. He was born in 1778, the son of a Cornish woodcarver, and was predominantly self-educated, in fact left school at sixteen; by 1812 Davy was Director of the Royal Institution and "already regarded as Britain's leading scientist."

His story includes the other reigning panjandrums of electromagnetic experiments. He knew Andre-Marie Ampère (who made a gift to Davy of a then-mysterious substance Davy analyzed and introduced as *iodine:* "It soon became, after opium, the most useful item in the medical pharmacopoeia"). He seized on Volta's discovery of the battery, and used it to isolate sodium, strontium, barium, magnesium, and potassium. His protégé was Faraday, who created "not only the first electric motor, but, in essence, the first dynamo: he could generate power."

But Davy's curiosity was commodious, and he lectured—often to audiences of hundreds of general-interest-seekers—on mineralogy, "laughing gas," agriculture, geology, and more, and with a sideshow barker's sense of spectacle. He wrote of his "soda experiment" that "the globules flew with great velocity through the air in a state of vivid combustion, producing a beautiful effect of continued jets of fire."

He wrote poetry (Southey published some in 1799) and was acquainted with Coleridge, Wordsworth, Byron, Sir Walter Scott. It was Coleridge's early stated sense of science as a utopia shaper, science as humankind's liberator, that Davy took for his creed. (The line between the two realms of knowledge was not so resistant then.) And when Davy published his *Elements of Chemical Philosophy,* in 1812, one of its most swayed readers—already a zealous do-it-yourselfer of explosive powders, reeking beakers, and jolted newts—was twenty-year-old Percy Bysshe Shelley.

—who wrote, "What a mighty instrument would electricity be in the hands of him who knew how to wield it! . . . It will perhaps be possible at no very distant date to produce heat at will and to warm the most ungenial climates." He imagined a Montgolfier balloon, powered by the new galvanic battery, high over Africa: "As it glides silently over that hitherto unhappy country [it] would virtually emancipate every slave, and would annihilate slavery forever."

His poems would continue to be informed by these enthusiasms. *Queen Mab* (which appeared in 1813, the year after Davy's book) presents us with a chariot, a "magic car," that speeds with "burning wheels" through the heavens, leaving "a line of lightning" trailed behind it—driven, we'd say, by electrical engine. Six years later, in his *Prometheus* sequence, the universe's electrical power is shown to be the vehicle for a universal love (along the lines of Davy's idea of matter as systematized electrical force); if lightning can be mastered, it follows that love can be turned to the purposes of a Shelleyan radicalized good will. And then we'd have a world in which

> The lightning in his slave; heaven's utmost deep
> Gives up her stars, and like a flock of sheep
> They pass before his eyes, are numbered, and roll on!
> The tempest is his steed, he strides the air;
> And the abyss shouts from her depths laid bare,
> Heaven, hast thou secrets? Man unveils me; I have none.

But when we join him, he's still a precocious child, engaged in using a home-made "electrical plaister" to cure his sister's chilblains. Here he is again, terrorizing the household with a portable stove poured full of inflammable liquids—*I will take a birch to his buttercream arse until it's as rose as a rat's nose* . . . He's set fire to the butler.

At Eton, in 1808, he electrifies a doorknob—as well as his tutor, who's flung like a rucksack at the farther wall. He sets a tree on fire, using gunpowder of his own admixture. Employing a local tinker's help, he builds his own steam engine; on a Sunday, in the middle of silent devotion, it explodes, at the cost of half of a clerestory window and that whole year's store of cheeses. Dr. Bethel claims to have found him one day sitting like a chiseled heathen idol in the middle of a fly-blue circle of spirit-flame, attempting to conjure the devil. "It was, I think, an instance of like calling like."

Oxford, on the whole, is no more congenial to his zeals. Of a session on mineralogy: the lecturer "talked about nothing but stones, stones, stones, stones, nothing but stones, and so drily." He's constructing, he confides to schoolfriend Thomas Jefferson Hogg, a great electrical kit, "or rather combination of kits, that would draw down from the sky an immense volume of electricity, the whole ammunition of a mighty thunderstorm." And then? With the sky in a jar—*then?* Serfs unshackled, icebergs towed into quays for the easy confecting of sherbets for the whole of the Empire, women's bodices willingly unribboned in the shadows of the ivy trellises, rheum and lameness vanquished at the application of surgical sparks!

Twenty-five years later, Hogg sets down the look of Shelley's room:

> Books, boots, papers, shoes, philosophical instruments, clothes, pistols, linen, crockery, ammunition, and phials innumerable, with money, stockings, prints, crucibles, bags and boxes were scattered on the floor and in every place, as if the young chemist, in order to analyse the mystery of creation, had endeavored first to construct the primeval chaos. The tables, and especially the carpet, were already stained with large spots of various hues, which frequently proclaimed the agency of fire. An electrical machine, an air-pump, the galvanic trough, a solar microscope, a small glass retort above an argand lamp.

Was there a Yorick-like skull to brood upon? A teakettle straining to power a goose quill sharpening machine?

A dozen times, the tyro experimenter treats Hogg to an overflux of eggy, miasmatic gases.

He entices Hogg to fiercely crank the electric battery's handle, and then he conducts its energy into himself—his hair like a field of wheat that's wildly rising from genuflection.

And once, Hogg hears a small *kablooey* and rushes horrified down the hall: there's Shelley, charred like a marshmallow head to toe, his shirt askew and the shirttails smoking, the stench of the netherworld settling like a wilted wreath around him, and a smile as wide and as white as a meadow of clover beaming through it all.

The air is acrackle with promise.

The Whole of a Person's Nature

It was raining, thin but steady, and I suddenly remembered—*it must be thirty-five years!*—The Weather Master. What daffy conjoinings of neural linkup conjured him back from oblivion?

He could thicken a lucid June sky into a threatening tornado, with the ease of someone whipping up egg whites—"Look! A tornado! Where the dingblast did THAT come from!"—and his henchmen would make their getaway in the ensuing confusion. Always, they'd be frantically heisting money bags shrilly imprinted with the dollar sign: $. And always, meteorology was accessory to the crime—a sudden drought, a ruinous hailstorm, a gale wind dispersing the topsy-turvied representatives of the law.

Back then, the civic peace of comic books was monthly interrupted by a succession of errant geniuses whose one defining circumstance—whose reason for existence and entire mode of being—was implied in their public monikers: The Wheel Master (flying buzzsaw wheels cutting bank vaults open, or flamethrower wheels fending off police troops, etc.), The Raven (commanded all of the birds of the air to do his evil bidding, and also flew jet planes of various bird shapes), Mr. Night ("What's this! It's high noon but the city streets are as dark as if it's midnight!").

Two of Batman's recurrent nemeses, The Joker and The Penguin, have entered the starry realm of popular culture legend, but the roll call of the similarly one-dimensional villains of that era is legion: Volcano Man, Inferno, Doctor Freeze, The Lizard Lady

("She's cold-blooded, boys!"), The Calendar Man, Mirage-O, Captain Canine... Of his lesser-known antagonists, for example, Batman once matched wits against that trio The Fox, The Shark, and The Vulture—they had the animal heads of Egyptian gods and the cheap huge-shouldered suits of common hoodlums. One of my favorites is The Fisherman, who stymied Blackhawk for seven pages, appearing in an aerial boat and hooking up loot with amazingly perfect flycasts.

The heroes, of course, were always also done in monochromatic portraiture (like all of that bat relentlessness: the Bat Cave, the batbelt, the batmobile, Bat Girl, Bat Dog, Bat Mite, the jillion-megawatt bat signal that turned the whole sky over Gotham City into his scallopy logo . . .) and the war of Good against Bad was frequently emblemized, in comicdom's stark manner, by setting Trait against Trait: so that in October 1956, in *Showcase* number four with the Joe Kubert art, in his debut appearance, The Flash ("the scarlet speedster," "the fastest man alive," "the human thunderbolt") is on the trail of Turtle Man, "the slowest man on Earth," who speaks annoyingly with ellipses between each two consecutive words.

This was a world defined by criminal endeavor, by explosion, knife, pursuit, and yet—those monolithic signifiers that meant, and *were,* the whole of a person's nature never failed us.

By my tokens shall ye know me . . . and unmistakably.

What a comforting world.

That year, they herded all of the third and fourth grade classes drag-footed into assembly hall, and treated us to a hokey twenty minutes of filmic caveat, *The World of Willie and Wendy Warning,* a woodenly-done precursor to the spiffier "just say no" films of the nineties.

For Willie and Wendy, the daily walk to school was fraught

with hidden danger, some of it forthright, like a speeding sedan through a red light, some more guileful. It turned out seemingly friendly strangers, smiles momentarily snapped to their faces like Mr. Potato Head features, slowly drove their inconspicuous station wagons around the blocks alert for the chance to work evil on the soft wax of our child bodies.

I don't know with what value the assembly halls of Dunkens Corners and Dipdale took such cautionary drama, but in Chicago we took it *seriously*. One March the mounded snows of an especially malevolent winter receded and under them, in one of the tatty gatherings of trees that they call forest preserves, a luckless birder found the Gurney brothers, seven and ten, who'd been missing since January: their toes had been sliced off, and one his nose, and exes cut into their sides, like grill-marks seared on beef.

Who did it? It took a month to find the toes in a paper bag in the freezer deeps of "Uncle Andy's" pedal-powered ice cream wagon. He was a neighborhood fixture, "so *gentle* with children," "like one of the family," "a saintly smile, it made you feel good all over." Every spring, as dependable as the return of the washed-out city robins, Uncle Andy began his rounds; he was readying for the new year's when the cops appeared with their warrant. For me—I was seven then too—the most scarifying part was that they never did find the nose. It floated tentacled through my nightmares.

And it could happen closer to home, we found that out, we pieced it up from whispered innuendo and hindsight. A woman who lived on our block, in fact it was the corner brownstone fourplex, whipped her six-year-old daughter's thigh-backs with a naked wire hanger while the girl was drugged, supposedly to claim an ex-husband had done it, and so garner on-the-scene support from some prospective new beau. "A *monster*," I heard my mother say, then she hushed when I walked in the room.

A monster, yes—and like the ones I knew, the werewolf and

the vampiress, the more horrific for passing as any ordinary citizen. She dressed like my mother, she did her hair like my mother's, she'd grin hello to me, and I'd see the daughter—Rita, I think: a grade behind me in school—at recess, playing at jacks or jump rope unconcernedly in the community roar.

How close *could* this uncertainty encroach? Did it hide like a parasite inside my own parents—sucking plugged to a blood-stuffed nub and biding its time? I jiggled my face in the round of a polished tablespoon. It told me we were frighteningly polymorphous sentiences, adrift on winds of cosmic whim. I stretched my face like play goo, I contracted it into a dime-sized facial fist.

In the last beshatted days when the marriage was finally, thank God, breaking apart—and breaking painfully, like operation stitches ripped undone—we both became "different people." I've talked to Morgan since, so know she felt it too. Those children's "action dolls" with the plastic heads you can jerkily swivel around so the copyrighted hero becomes some equally copyrighted skull-faced demon?—we would vacuously smile our way through parties, sip wine normally with our mutual friends, then hit the car and on the way home spit at each other like alleycats working up bloodlust.

This isn't accurate really. It's not that our selves were divided in two—our selves were splintered *uncountably* by the daily emotional damage. We were votaries at the altar of Confusion, and anything "really" "me" was about the size of a flake of fish food, tossed and then lost in the psychic chop.

One night a "me" said something to one of "her," I don't remember what, but I do remember—loaded into all five of my senses, down to the upholstery weave—how Morgan, my light, my petal, was suddenly raging as the car roared up the Austin, Texas, outback darkness, suddenly raging and flinging open the car door, sixty miles an hour of black wind shearing along her one flung leg and grabbing her hair like a mugger, raging, cursing not only me but her own sad life in words the speed yanked out of her by the roots while I clung to an arm and she clung to the distant rattling handle.

What I remember next—it's later that night, I'm alone now, and I'm dazedly walking the night off, in the rain. It strafes my cheeks. It muddles everything, who's wrong, who's right, who wakes in my brain in the mornings. Now if only I *had* The Weather Master to fight, to be the yang for, while his simple greedy yin romped all amok . . . If he were here in his primary colors, wouldn't I find myself analogously reduced—or is it elevated? sanctified?—to be one clear pure thing.

1842. "Charles Dickens, Esquire" is on board the steam-packet *Britannia* en route to the United States. It's night, it's past eleven o'clock, and Dickens studies the nautical dark and its texture:

> Even when the hour, and all the objects it exalts, have come to be familiar, it is difficult, alone and thoughtful, to hold them to their proper shapes and forms. They change with the wandering fancy; assume the semblance of things left far away; put on the well-remembered aspect of favourite places dearly loved; and even people them[selves] with shadows. Streets, houses, rooms; figures so like their usual occupants, that they have startled me by their reality, which far exceeded, as it seemed to me, all power of mine to conjure up the absent; have, many and many a time, at such an hour, grown suddenly out of objects with whose real look, and use, and purpose, I was as well acquainted as with my own two hands.

And then it's daybreak: light uncomplicates that scene. The pennants flapping like a string of trapped grouse. The exact silhouette of a funnel against the albumeny Atlantic sky. His knuckle-ridged hands on the rail.

For a moment, everything's totally and only its dictionary definition. For a moment, a man can believe that he is—that anyone is—one unit of a Unity.

First there is a Wholeness. Then the universe is created from—created *away from*—this Wholeness. "In the beginning," let's say, is God. And then: "God divided the light from the darkness."

This is how it always happens. Let's say, as the Omaha Indians say, that "at the beginning all things were in the mind of Wakonda, all creatures," but "they were seeking a place where they could come into bodily existence," and so "they descended to the earth." In Tibet, "the Essence of the Five Primordial Elements" produces an egg, a great egg, and then "eighteen eggs came forth from the yolk of that great egg."

Creation *is* division. Just diversify your models, and then your models of models, far enough away from their ur-mythic, Edenic origin or from Plato's "World of Ideal Forms," and what you have is Darwin: all that rending, all that saline reek and gnash. (A torn-off frog head at the pond—is that part of the Wholeness?) You have the fracas and thrash of any two struggling lovers.

This is our torment, maybe under the daily eruptions of salary-anger, alimony-negotiation, and politics-swagger, this is our built-in, bedrock torment: that we lead the lives of essentially fractioned creatures in an essentially fractioned cosmos.

Oh but isn't that our comfort as well?—the thought of some Totality or Source or Matrix, call it what you will, Germplasm, Goddess-womb, from which we appear and into which we disappear, remixing.

Call it The One. Call it "Numbakulla, whose name means 'always existing' or 'out of nothing.'" Call it The Waters. Yes: in *Genesis*, "God moved upon the face of the waters" even before the creation of light. For the Omaha, "the earth was covered with water" *already*—prior to the first breath of the first words of the story.

What did it matter to me? What did anything that fuckheaded conceptual matter to me?

I'd been hurt by a woman, and I'd dished hurt straight back at her, some *so* exquisite it might be called invidiousness, and some just unadorned meanspirited low-blow lobs of foul-mouth. Now I only wanted the needlepoint rain of a dregs-end Austin, Texas, summer night to wash me clean.

Because it can, at least in a limited way, if you open yourself to its powers. And I was open. I gaped; a bamboo leaf beat free of its stalk could have floated out of the parking lot on Forty-fifth at Red River and flimmered right through a hole in my breast and out the other side.

I couldn't have told you a thing about The Waters, primal this or primal that. But I had the rain. The sun came up, and still it rained, and still I headed steadily into it. It parted. I wouldn't stop until *it* faltered and stopped, but it didn't. I kept on thinking I could trace it to the place where rain was something entire—rain before it fell, before the world—and I could enter.

My Week Aboard a UFO!!!

A bitter Wichita, Kansas, winter day. The air is hard, and everything tempted to appear in an afternoon hour or two of tepid sunlight moves with recognition of that hardness, circles overhead as if turning an adamant millwheel (crows), or raises a lavish tail the shape—and I would swear the brittleness—of the ice-fronds on a window (a squirrel).

Only the cardinal feasting at my neighbor's backyard feeder seems to maintain its usual flickering movement. All of the other birds about it peck and squabble and drably rustle their bodies with what looks like, in comparison, arthritis. The cardinal, though—that *scorch*—is too quick for my eye. I miss so much, its motion seems to be all disconnected jerkiness, as if I'm only given every second frame of a reel of film. In fact, the cardinal *is* the lesson of motion pictures: the human eye is fallible, and can't keep up, and invents. But the movies are paced to match that invention, while the cardinal supersedes it.

The cardinal says: what the universe is, is mainly hillocks of sumptuous curlicued film on the cutting-room floor we'll *never* see. Dark matter. Infrared. The dreams in the skull a finger-width away from yours on the pillow. Flying saucer abductions—so often repressed. Satanic abuse—repressed. The puff of a moment in which we opened our eyes and their first light filled the residual gum of the womb the way light travels through a pane of stained glass, saying its stories of glory in an untranslatable language . . .

All, on the cutting-room floor.

The Missing Link. *Cut.* Amelia Earhart. *Cut.* The taste of our own tongues. *Cut.* The carefully hidden love life of the cuckold's wife, in a series of gaudily, honkytonkily decorated motel rooms usually highlighted (faucets, phone rim) in a *très faux* mother-of-pearl, so that her fancy calls back each of those rooms in its place along a lovely nacred curve like that of the local museum's chambered nautilus. *Cut, cut, cut.* Dropped out of the line of ongoingness we live along.

The cardinal's motion is snippets. And I know if we could see its movement as fluidly as it happens, as it *really* happens—if we could see with the time geology keeps, or the stars—then there would be no secrets from us, no puzzles, not the subatomic rhumba lessons by which the physical universe is kept in its version of order, not the fierce pinwheeling outward of the galaxies, not the intimate greed- and lust-noise of the fourplex human heart, no not the secrets of the hummingbird's tongue or the whale's vagina or any of the antimatter thereof would be opaque to us, and we would know what the gods know, which would be an example of contents overmuch for their container; we would explode, from the burden of wholeness.

Dropped out of the line of ongoingness . . .

Was the night especially eldritch? Did its moon bob in a wisp of skyey fish-milt, and did shadows splay across the land? We don't know. What we know is that it *was* night, in the Vale of Heath, South Wales, and "a certain Mr. Rhys," who with his fellow worker Llewellyn was driving a string of horses back to the farm, remarked that he heard fiddles nearby and thought he'd seek them out, to "have a dance." Llewellyn returned alone. Rhys never returned. A thorough daylight search of the area failed to turn up Rhys or any clue, and soon Llewellyn was suspected of his murder.

A week had already passed when a local farmer wise in the ways of the mysteries persuaded a group—Llewellyn was included—to revisit the scene of the disappearance under his sage direction. "There Llewellyn heard the music. His foot was on the edge of a fairy ring." Anyone touching Llewellyn could also hear music, "and saw a crowd of figures dancing in the ring, with Rhys among them." Still with one foot in the world of humankind, and with the rest of the party anchoring him in that world, Llewellyn snatched at Rhys, and over the dancer's squealing protests dragged him out of the ring.

Rhys somberly blinked the haze from his eyes. "It seemed to him he had been dancing only five minutes or so," goes the story.

Lost time.

One hundred and fifty years later it happens again, although in the language of 150 years later. At night, on her way home from a class she teaches in urban planning, Elizabeth Ultman's car stops dead. "I don't mean it sputtered and slowed down. First it's going fifty miles an hour, then *bingo* it's stopped." This happens between one small Wisconsin town and another. There's no one around. There's *nothing* around. "And then there's a light, and I'm out of the car, and fizzing up through the light as if I'm an Alka-Seltzer."

Aboard the saucer, she's prodded and rayed and electroded—not ungently—by a team (a pod? a pirate gang? a technical crew?) of the ancient-seeming, yet fetally-featured, beings one reads so much about in the literature of contactees. "Then everything misted over, and I woke up back on Earth"—she's found, a little disheveled, a lot disoriented, walking directionlessly on a backwoods road in downstate Illinois. It's seven days since her parents reported her missing.

"I thought I was in their ship for two or three hours, it couldn't have been more than that."

Or multiple personality disorder—two or more coterminous, separate personalities "alive" in the same fraught mind. Each has its detailed history, networks of friends, and distinctive speech. There might be a four-year-old child and then, in immediate segue, a slinky bar girl—both of them whole and convincing. Usually, they "have no recollection of their intervening 'sleep,' picking up mid-speech or action at the exact point at which they were interrupted, the hiatus ranging from minutes to several years." Lost time. Lost people.

The power the state takes on in Orwell's *1984* is precisely that of the cutting room: an office makes a decision, say at the Ministry of Truth, and somebody "unexists"; it's not that someone vanishes, but that he *never was;* is scissored out of the fabric and is scissored out of the history of the fabric. Someone never traced the fluted neck and cool paunch of that sea-green crystal budvase in the kitchen window, someone never ran his hand across you, trembling, *here* and even *here.* The air reorganizes: someone never ambled through it. Stains and stinks reorganize. The molecules undo their winding conga lines, and then redo them anew. Australopithecus never existed: the grasses reshuffle. That photograph doesn't exist: the wedding-ring line on your finger tans over.

I'm thinking about the painful weekly witnessing of the marriage of my friends Celeste and Eddie as it further shattered. The atmosphere of an easy social evening in their company would crawl across your scalp. And then "Oh you can kiss my ass," and worse; the make-you-cringe appearance of invective like the living toads we hear about sometimes, freed from the heart of a rock. Those scenes were finally no surprise any longer; so neither was, when they first got around to trying it out in public, like a name for the only child they'd ever have together, the word *divorce.*

For that bad while, the people I knew as "Celeste" and "Eddie" were gone, replaced by eerily look-alike changeling friends, who might sport her hoop earrings, his alpaca coat, might even be robotically repeating the conversational tropes I knew to be an

"Eddiehood" or a "Celesteism"—yes, but uttered with the necessarily shaken-empty grimness we work up to face adversity; or with the manic overkill of an amateur clown; until nothing was left of the actual "them" except jewelry and a wardrobe. "When I'm with him," she said, "I try to be only a hanger for my clothes."

And as they disappeared in front of me—in space—they made each other disappear in time as well. She *wasn't* there, he swore, the day he such-and-so-forth'ed. Yeah?—she sure the goddam hell *was,* buddy: *he's* the one who never thus-and-furthermore'd. The fundament of Memory collapsing. Each of them, meditatively studying a face in the bathroom mirror: Who *is* that? Brandishing the shears by which we recognize a petty functionary at the Ministry of Truth. "A new future," Bernard Lewis says in his *History: Remembered, Recovered, Invented,* "requires a different past." The mountains of certainty? . . . Snowmelt. Static.

"It *happened,*" Elizabeth Ultman says as the final line of her narrative—says it quietly, half to herself, so says it all the more persuasively for lack of histrionics. Do I believe in these other-planetary bipeds with their slightly-more-than-Terran rockets and medical probes, and their oh-so-very-human curiosity? Do I think they ride the skies in swooping paisley-shape space vehicles, and intervene, with peoplecatcher tongs and great hypnotic eyes, in the muddled affairs of Mineral Wells, Wisconsin? I think not.

But *something's* happening out there, swarming auditoriums at conventions of the UFO-abducted—more each year, and more emphatic. Something's feeding the surface ire of my lawyer-counseled, loggerheads friends. Whatever it is, however deep it surges from, we've all been evicted from Eden, I mean the womb—the original cutting-room slice—and, even before that, been the bird- and lizard-us which wouldn't stay unchanging, which impelled us up the protein/protean process of evolving that's also a process of always jettisoning a former self, until the nurse's casual slap at the just-delivered bloodslicked toosh announced our welcome into a world of "God" and "love" and the first tick lost from our personal clock of mortality.

The police call. Midnight, 1 A.M. Mrs. Ultman? We've found your daughter. Yes ma'am. She seems all right, but also she seems to have come through some trying ordeal.

"The brain's chief function is selective forgetting."

(Otherwise presumably we'd go mad from detail overload.)

That's the seductive promise of Big Brother: give control unto me, and I'll do the work of your brain for you. Signing up as a lifer in the military, entering the convent: handing over the sticky bother of decision-making.

By this criterion, Erving Goffman classifies together institutions seemingly so diverse as TB sanitaria and POW camps. And in his book *Asylums* he presents a study of the means (the insistence on uniforms, the partial or total replacement of personal doodads from one's former life, renaming—or maybe numbering—etc.) by which identity is erased—"assaults upon the self," as Goffman says. Lost people. Business as usual—*cut*—at the Ministry of Truth.

Of course the first thing clipped from the record is inevitably a competing Truth; the successors to Akhnaton knocked his face from statues and his name from cartouches and other inscriptions *tens of thousands* of times, a monumental (or, more literally, de-monumental) total tonnage of undone stone.

And often, chance alone conducts some nullifying labor for the Ministry of Truth, on its behalf: it's chance, bad chance of a particularly irksome sort, that Pieter Brueghel's last gift to the world, *The Triumph of Truth,* is lost to us. We only have Karl Van Mander's after-the-fact account of 1604, in his anecdotal book of "the lives of the most illustrious painters of the Lowlands," and here

Van Mander says, as his ending lines of the Brueghel entry, "He did one more painting, entitled *The Triumph of Truth*. It was, he said, his best work." And then he died—in 1569, about fifty.

What was it like? It was large, no doubt. (The earlier *The Triumph of Death* is almost four feet tall and over five feet long.) And it was . . . well, I imagine it existing to him as *The Tempest* did to Shakespeare—as a grace note, a diminuendo ever-rippling into a kind of patterned awareness that makes cohesive sense of the gala fury that's long preceded it; as a swan song, as the music flowering poignantly out of that lifted slender throat the way the rose is an explosion at the mouth of its stem.

I imagine this is exactly the cosmology Big Brother and his officialdom most fervently need to obliterate: a triumph of retrieval, of the wayward, and the condemned, and the abandoned, of the ostracized and the taboo, of every castoff clipping, glued back by the force of Brueghel's vision into the read text of the world: a Truth that *is* the Truth because—so simple, really—it's Totality. (I see the smoke plumes of a million bonfired books respooling back into their volumes, char made whole, the very oxidation halted and healed, and those pages once again awaiting an absently licked finger.)

I imagine him, he's forty-nine, he's standing in the attic workshop light, it's dawn, as if the world itself has just opened its eyes, and he's considering this painting, this still-unresolved and all-things-possible half-completed painting, as a universe he'd like to enter (soon, I suppose, he will), and touch the artfully positioned russets and dove-grays of his grand design as if they truly were the kitchen ladles and skinned-clean market hares and worn-but-durable saddle pommels and catches of herring and lace trim and alembics and buttons and harvesting scythes of what we call, for lack of anything clearer and finer, "the real world."

Here, in this canvas's forming landscape, all of his earlier paintings, which were isolated units of his life, return—and recombine in harmony. Here, the disappointed hunters silently print their way home through the snow; and the Tower of Babel impossibly rises skyward, looking like a honeycomb half-swiped to a convoluted stump by a bear; and the chopped-apart bodies of infants (this would be *The Slaughter of the Innocents*) are tossed to the snow like food for the scavenging dogs (there are scavenging dogs); and, in their milky sea-chop, Icarus's scissoring legs are a failing call for attention below the vast untenanted sky.

They're here, they're all here, not one is forgotten.

And isn't it a fact that nothing *does* disappear from the submost annals? Every-breath-we-take-contains-some-atoms-breathed-by-Julius-Caesar etc. Eidetic memory. Aren't we elements out of star and stone, in newer combination? All of those tabloid-belovéd dogs returning to master (the champion, Bobbie, lost in Wolcott, Indiana, and trekking over three thousand miles home to Silverton, Oregon). Doesn't the force behind What Is—despite all of its fog and casual invention—hold on tenaciously?

Timothy Leary on senility: "It improves long-term memory—in walking to the kitchen I remember fighting another kid when we were four, and all of my grade school teachers, and my first date."

The ancient Jewish fortress Masada "is not mentioned in the rich Rabbinic literature. Jewish tradition knows nothing of Masada . . . [and] even the Hebrew spelling of the name is conjectural." But nineteen hundred years later, archeology "remembered" the site. "Today, Israeli armored corps recruits are sworn in on Masada. It is not uncommon to see one saying his sunrise prayers in the world's oldest extant synagogue."

Isn't DNA a "living fossil"? Speaking of which . . . the Dallas Area Rapid Transit Authority halted work on a subway tunnel "because its tunnel-boring machines released pockets of methane gas that had been trapped in the rock when ancient giant sea worms decayed." A cockroach is the planet remembering perfectly, down to the spiracle, its earlier self. It's remembered itself for 250 million years this way—without alteration.

Bad pennies show up again, mnemonics recall the primary colors, and Wordsworth's daffodils won't remain in psychological banishment, no, they "flash" and "dance" etherically but viably from the paved-over levels of mind.

"Think, sweet."

"I can't, I *told* you, I can't!"

A hand on her head. A mother's hand. "The doctor says."

Elizabeth Ultman squirms on her parents' living-room couch. So many days.

"I don't *care* what the doctor . . ." Stops. / The doctor. / Doctors. / A medical table. / Exam. / "No."

"Honey . . . ? What, dear? Easy."

"No!"

"Elizabeth? Henry, come in here! Hold her! *Elizabeth!*"

"NO! NO! NO!"

Shakespeare's last play is *The Tempest*. By a surface coincidence, Brueghel's last completed painting (that we still have) is *The Storm at Sea*.

A ship is in distress, in darkly frightening heaves of ocean as tall as its sails. A whale, its mouth agape—its open mouth the entrance to a monstrous, meat-red sleeve—is drawing near. The sailors have vainly thrown a barrel its way, to divert it; and have vainly (this was the lore of the day) poured oil of castoreum over the clashing waters, to frighten it. But it isn't frightened. It isn't diverted. It charges on, powered by primal red.

Next, they'll make an offering of Jonah. He gets flung to the waves, and swallowed into those alien coils, and taken on the mysterious journey.

The whale—the mother ship—diving deep into the only outer space of the time.

✦

It also happened to me.

In the days of my own divorce, when, out of the breach of mild disaffection, the bully-boys Chaos and Enmity stepped forth to declare their reign, I felt myself change, in becoming their loyal subject. Not forever changed, I think; but changed so long as they held sway. And some "essential Albert" slipped with frequency out of my grip like a sliver of soap in the dirty bathwater she and I had made of things.

I'd look at Morgan—who *was* this? She'd moved out, and on the days when we convened to sign a paper or haggle spiritedly over some grain of our mutual possessions, I might slide a side-long glance her way as she'd be counting dogeared paperback books or tarnished silver, and wonder who this prim, itinerary-taking stranger could be, as if I were a child who'd been led without preparation to the cult house of an angry god. Who *was* this angry priestess of his? I was too small; I couldn't imagine.

There must be an army of strangers waiting in each of us. Replacement selves.

What happened on that wickedly chilly December night in 1926 when Agatha Christie—thirty-six then, and with seven respectable mystery novels behind her—disappeared from the world for eleven days? We know that her recentmost novel had met unfavorable reviews, that her mother had died, that her husband, Colonel Archibald Christie, had lately fallen in love with a younger woman and wanted divorce; that she was sleeping poorly, eating erratically, moving herself and her furniture dazedly around their splendiferous country house at Sunningdale in Berkshire; and that, on the morning after her vanishing, her Morris two-seater was found slid halfway down a bank of iced grass, with its bonnet stuck in a clump of bushes.

And then . . . ? We don't know. Whatever happens, happens in the land of Bermuda Trianpleish speculation, it flies to whatever place Hemingway's legendary early manuscripts went to, in the suitcase that was stolen off the train that day . . . The chronicles of unexplainable loss. Sometimes, the chronicles of equally mysterious return. Elaine Caplan, surgeon at New York's Animal Medical Center: "I once pulled a whole blanket out of a Doberman."

Evening. Dinner. The clinking of crystal. Eleven days after her disappearance, December 14, Agatha Christie is recognized by the headwaiter of the Hydropathic Hotel in North Yorkshire. She'd been there for the week and a half, a "visitor from South Africa" (she had registered under the name of her husband's mistress) who "seemed normal and happy, sang, danced, chatted with fellow guests, played billiards," and followed the florid newspaper coverage of the search for her (to the public's cost of three thousand pounds) with the same detached interest the other guests gave it. Wearing a plain gray cardigan and green knit skirt the night of her disappearance, and with a few pounds in her purse, she was found dressed stylishly now and with three hundred pounds upon her.

Amnesia? Nervous breakdown? Publicity ploy (in fact her next book doubled the best of her earlier sales figures)? A spiteful and highly ornate attempt to bring her husband's philandering into the open? Even—part one of a fumbled plan to murder (or sully the name of) the other woman? We don't know. She never 'fessed up. All we can do is picture Agatha Christie–prime and Agatha Christie–parallel: one steps into her Morris and drives herself into the night like a sentence back into its ink; the other steps out.

"Albert—?"

Where was I? Who was this? My mother.

My father had died, and this was my mother, and we were sitting out the ritual *shiva* mourning at her house.

"I'm okay . . ."

My father had died, the same month the divorce was final. A week before, he'd loaned me the money to carry me through the basic bucks that kind of breakage costs, and now in the other room my sister was explaining to my niece about "up to heaven" and "with *his* mommy now" and the rest of it. And as for *my* mother . . . the truth is, it was easier being strong for her (or that's the way I needed to see it: that I was "strong," "for her") than it was to be strong for myself in my alternately broken- and hard-hearted shambles.

But such strength is expensive, and he wasn't here any longer to offer me loans. This is the only way I can say it: I must have put my prime-self up for hock for a while, pawned myself, in some required metaphysical way, and left the Albert-parallel dealing with grief maturely. Reciting the mourner's *kaddish* unfalteringly.

And what was this image that everybody recognized on the TV screen? This scraggled smoky Y.

"I'm just going out for a walk for a minute. I'll be right back."

The trail the spaceship *Challenger* made, exploding.

Maybe some of its import did sink in. Outside, I had the crazy feeling the sky was coming apart above me, coming apart then massing back closed. A symbol, I suppose, that I read into the outside cosmos—of my own, interior phasing in and out. Is this the tumult that the saucer spotters tell themselves they see?

Or it was the *Challenger*'s psychic disturbance of the national air. Or my sister was right, and heaven had opened up and was closing.

Those are the kinds of things you think at such moments. My breath was frantic, then calmed. January. Anything I said wore a mask: my own breath.

Yes, or maybe it was just that a cardinal flickered above me in passage, and I filed away its ungraspable movement.

Anyway—*some* confusion of wings, that blurred the still clear morning.

Keepers of the Flame

Two-Els

They don't know *how,* in an A-security ward, he finagled himself a matchbook. But he did; he set his hair on fire—again—and here he is now, thrashing violently over the rec room floor, a nightmare's nightmare come to wakeful life.

I wish I could write about him. Even here, amidst the veteran excrement eaters, lesion pickers, and zero-eyed starers, he's known as The Legend. And when he's doused and forcibly sedated, and a fidgety calm returns, we see the rec room television bears the image of a holocaustal fire in some riot-torn downtown; I could swear it's an infant that the jumpy 'copter camcorder footage catches being pitched off a roof.

Somebody bearing witness to this, in an essay. Someone adequately finding an interior heat that's equal to this contagion of madness and rage. I've done that essay, I've written that poem, before.

But now, today, the subject is the sifted-down ash of a mild regret that grabs me by the jacket lapels and shakes me with a wiry strength, imploring me to tell its story—and, to be honest, I need to hearken to this.

When I look carefully, I see that the jacket it grabs me by is a baggy vinyl windbreaker that I wore all through the autumn of 1956. I'm eight. The air is . . . listen: "I asked many people what scent first came to mind at the mention of autumn. To most, I think, it was the smell of burning leaves" (E. W. Teale, *Autumn Across America, 1956*).

The air is signifiers, is something stirring chthonically in the memory hookup. Everything else—the overpowering sweep of human drama with its winged awards and its ambulance wail— is sacrificed now, to be this smoke that rises from an oildrum like a pillar, one of hundreds of thousands of pillars that bear up the sky of that year.

"Hearken," I just wrote. "Amidst." I'm trying to think of the little things that leave us, almost unnoticed. Hairnets carded four-for-a-dime in a tray at the local five-and-ten.

"Whence," I say aloud, and see it flimmer in the air. "Whence." "Lest." And "o'er." I like them. I look at them as if my gaze is high-beams freezing deer. There aren't many left on this urbanized side of the river, and it's staggering to see them a moment— almost an afterimage of their kind—before the spell breaks and they've melted back to darkness.

"Ergo." "Prithee." Back to the black of their ink.

A herd of them: "Whither." "Morrow." "Oft."

When an industry dies: subsidiary industries die.

The mail coach: the way station hostler.

1999—I don't think anybody's gung-ho into ashtray manufacture. Remember the giant kind, about the size of a washing machine, in festive colors and matched to the room's predominating notion: poodles; Chinese junks; pink elephants . . . ?

To the last, diehard practitioners of a craft, a heroism accrues. The woman who remembers the oral lexicon of quilters. The man who travels the country, renting queen bees. The smithy: a row of shoes—of upsilons—over his doorway.

"Melmac." "Dacron." "Naugahyde."

✦

My Uncle Lou—whose small and yet sustaining business seemed to me a fact of life, like the alternation of day and night, or the seasons—wasn't prescient enough to segue, when the time came, from producing accordion carrying cases to those for guitar: that flexibility hadn't been built in. And so he *was,* it turned out, a season: a decade of cultural taste.

I was six, seven. They had no children. He'd show me how to judge the slub of a bolt of silk. He'd run its powder-blue edge through his fingers like someone shyly, reverently playing with the negligee hem of a famous hothouse beauty. He let me wander the bolts—the pillars of an ancient city filled with dangerous shadow! He tried to explain the craft: Gots to heff goot heenges.

Then the silk was rayon. Then the quarterly catalogue was annual. When I was eight, he was dead, and Auntie Hannah said the doctor should write *foreclosure* under "cause of death."

That tidy wayside factory *is* an ancient city, nearly forty years ago lost to the wrecking ball. Completely unrecoverable, it is, in a sense, more distant than Pompeii or Chichen Itza.

I remember its rotary dial phone, a black substantiality with the *hereness* of a bowling ball. The ashtray in his customer showroom: two lime-green ceramic panthers bore an outstretched lime-green odalisque on their backs, who bore a lime-green basket for the ashes (it was taller than I was then). The tacked-up day-by-day wall calendar of the kind that, in the movies of the 1950s, always was having its pages blown away in a sudden gust of months—and so we'd know the arrow of time is like a snake: it sloughs.

I've trailed my hands with a breath-held wonder over the palm-sized terra cotta oil lamps of the Middle Bronze Age—corner-pinched to a clumsy quatrefoil shape—then held them close and viably breathed-in their odor from over four thousand years of human doing and undoing; but I've never yet found the lamp in the shape of a bellboy and a carhop holding hands (presumably after their shifts?) that lit my Auntie Hannah's face as she kneeled beside me, licking a Kleenex, then wiping the tear tracks off my cheeks.

I remember for him the gradual dissolution of the business was a quiet, interior sadness. He could see it happening order after order, in diminishment, over ten years. Lucretius says, "The bronze statues at the city gates have right hands that are worn thin by the touch of travellers who greet them in passing." That's the way my uncle went, in barely discernible increments.

But he had a partner: the company was called Two-Els. At Uncle Lou's funeral, Laszlo stood there radiating rage; I thought of the Pillar of Fire, out of my Bible in Hebrew school.

In Europe—back in the Old Country—he had been Laszlo, cutter of fine cloth to the Duke and to the rabbinate, and in the dressing chambers of ladies of high estate, who had him drape the gold-shot damask over breasts that not even their own physicians ever touched—he, Laszlo! Now he hated the world. He hated my Uncle Lou's so uncomplainingly succumbing to the world. My uncle's death was felt by Laszlo to be a betrayal of their partnership.

I see that now. But then—? I was eight, a kid in a vinyl windbreaker secretly tucking a soggy Swiss Warbler under his tongue.

(Do you remember them? "Ventriloquize Your Way to Popularity!" "Throw Your Voice!" And then a picture of some rascal punk adopting an angelic face while a workman lugged a great wooden crate on his back that was yelping *Help! Help! Let me out!!!*—a little-fingernail-width of reed you bought for a penny, hopefully sloshed around in your saliva for a while, vainly striving for one ventriloquial poot, then threw disgustedly away . . .)

Not that I thought of attempting any such tomfoolery that day. I only wanted something hidden and familiar I could bring to this, my first true being-admitted to the world of adult grief. In fact, I don't remember feeling grief. I don't remember feeling any loss: I was eight, I was happily stupid and eight.

What I do remember is how Laszlo suddenly ran to the side of the grave with a guitar in his hand, interrupting the service. He flung it showily, viciously to the ground and started stomping on it—energetic, moonleap stomps—the goddam, the accursed, guitar: the destroyer of family businesses!

It was only string and splinters by the time my father and two older cousins subdued him. *That's* the picture I've brought with me from the scene of my aunt in the throes of her bereavement.

It was thirty years later before I understood, before I *really* understood. And when I looked down into my father's casket—his carrying case, I guess you could say—I unaccountably heard, from nowhere, Gots to heff goot heenges.

✦

A Smaller and Bearable Voice

And this is the way they gouge out an eye with a spoon in Rwanda. In Bosnia. In any cellar storeroom where the door is chained against media supersnooping in the cities of the Mississippi Valley. This is the way they make you talk, the tooth-edged clip around your nipple, the match at your balls.

But this is personal. For *general* devastation, a sniper eyried in the belltower is efficient, or—for easiest and largest-scale effect— the mere withholding from a populace of any material goods: this guarantees not just the passing of a life, but of a way of life.

I wish I could write about this. The child floating in an inner tube in the turd-clogged drinking stream of a village.

"Village," I said, but Dog Bone Hill is shacks of cardboard and garbage-bag plastic. The Bigwig deals business from a junked van that, when the tide slimes in, can be up past its headlights in dead rats.

This is no anomalous knot of human misery: this is the future. This is the pent-up, conflagration-under-the-braincap, savage strength of the future, knit tight, unassuageable. "The world," says Michael Vlahos, a U.S. Navy payroll brain, "is not following us. It is going in many directions. Do not assume that democratic capitalism is the last word in human social evolution."

Everything altering. Of course. You can't be alive in the future without consuming the dead. Propulsion *is* change.

And once, their people practiced daily rituals of magisterial power: the masks of cowrie and horn that the priestesses kept in the god-house, and the parade of initiates door to door with seeds in silver chalices, and the community lyrics sung at sun's set—fairy stories of birds on quests in the land of the ancestor High Ones.

Once. And now? ". . . not just the passing of a life, but of a way of life."

Or think of those New Guinea Stone Age people that we found unchanged for thousands of years, with suddenly one transistor radio traded to them.

The passing of which I mourn. I mean the radio. One, from when I was eight, a white and brick-red plastic Japanese product the size and shape of a deck of cards, I attended adoringly—so inept was its hesitant drizzleflurry-and-knucklecrack reception, it inspired extra devotion simply to be retained in the house at all. It had a small earplug, by which I could listen secretly; we were a *system*.

It's gone. I have it still, this relict one, but as *a class of object*: gone. The Automat: gone. The vinyl record: going. Drive-in movie theaters. Carbon paper. Now, today, the subject is a heart-pang as the dusts of yesterliving coat the moment.

In the basement of a library somewhere, someone is opening every drawer of the discontinued and un-updated, century-old card catalog that's scheduled for being trucked to the landfill—deeply inhaling a fraught aroma of cabinet oak and handled paper. Nicholson Baker opines that this card catalog is "in truth, the one holding that people (who enter a library) would be likely to have in common, to know how to use from childhood, even to love."

Silk stockings. "Rabbit-ear" TV antennae. Sectioned metal holders and their bottles of home-delivery milk . . .

. . . *Swiss Warblers.*

The ventriloquism tricks by which unbearable disappearance tries to speak to us in a smaller and bearable voice.

"Withal." "Tomfoolery." "Yclept." "Eftsoons." "Humdinger."

"Dasn't"—one of my father's words.

We dasn't _____ (here, you could fill in almost anything adventuresome by way of late hours or furtive consorting with strangers). He was fearful all his life, from love of us, as if some early proof of the terrors and vanishings the world can work had once so thoroughly demonstrated itself, he couldn't now cup our faces casually in his hands without remembering the brevity of flesh.

And yet this man helped search for bodies in the flooded mine, and helped patrol for plunderers after the gang war. He was known as someone to call if a building caught fire. Once, he walked between my sister and a frothing dog, an agitated thing with its rump-end cocked already for leaping. My father just stood there, as solid and empty and endlessly patient as a fortress door, he didn't give ground, he didn't give cause for attacking—and the dog slinked away.

Only *then* did he turn to Livia, she was four or five, and fall to his knees in front of her, his face so soft, so hopeless, it looked like a face of soap, dissolving in the turmoils of the day. He was no coward, he was simply a man who understood: we're x in a universal equation that's always looking to preface us with a minus sign.

"Hunky-dory," he'd say, if anything went well, or "copacetic." "Ixnay." "Toot sweet." "Yoo-hoo." "Moxie." "Ishkabibble." "Skedaddle."

Enough public ink is being lavished somewhere else right now on the loss of our "national identity," on the disappearance of "childhood" . . .

I'm going to remember the ill-lit dogpiss basement workroom where he fretted balanced answers every night from his account books, so the rent would be on time. Just that.

Just that, and the 1950s pea-green wholesale office desk down there. The round glass ashtray the size of a highball coaster (of the sort I once secretly slid in my fist, years later, for booted-up punching oomph in a bar fight). An old-fashioned adding machine with the bulk, the blunt industrial look, of a submarine's control panel out of World War II. Where would anyone go, today, for a virginal roll of its tape? For the pale box of blotting tissues he kept at the ready, alongside a lineup of extra bulbs for the fountain pens? For a slide rule?

Gone, irretrievably gone, a world for which we've yet to find the proper honorific set of obsequies.

Easier mourning these, than thinking of him directly.

Collar stays. Men's hankies. Yellow plastic shoehorns with the name of a local office supplies distributor on them.

"Obsequies."

The erasers I fancy especially: maybe a dozen kinds, as if to contend with error in a dozen different guises. I picture them dutifully, cartoonily erasing a row of figures off an onionskin page; and then the pad below it, and then the desk, and now the room is unroomed, and all of 1956 has ceased to exist, its last leaf burned and then even that one-leaf smoke erased, until only my father's face is left, and they take it from me feature by feature, until, like a pack of small rabid beasts, they even erase themselves, except of course for the memento one—the flat gray rolling disk and its leg of plastic bristle, for typewriter errors—I've placed in a drawer in a desk of my own, as if I could save an echo.

In fact, what current cosmology says—among its many hundreds of metaphorical applications—is that we *live in* an echo. We *are* an echo. We're nothing so much as the organized after-rumble of the original First Moment when space and time exploded out of no-space and no-time.

We're the densed-up blips on the chronological outpost-edge of 15 billion years of radiation—Arno Penzias and Robert Wilson heard it first, in 1965, while tracking Telstar with an ultrasensitive radio antenna. Although I fancy I've heard a version, myself: the cellophane-crackle that dollar-ninety-eight transistor radio provided as a preface, coda, and counterweight to all of human song.

So: echoes. Surely this explains nostalgia. Surely our common fondness for fossils—and I'm considering 1940s accordions and 1960's TV theme songs "fossils"—is a function of being compounded, ourselves, of souvenir *ur*-tumult from the Big Bang. *Its* smaller and bearable voice.

"Espy." "Forthwith." "Fiestaware."

Echoes. The tracks of a doe that one night seven years ago lightly patterned—like flowering plum on a Chinese vase—my neighbor's fresh cement. Now the deer are gone, and the sidewalk is saying this ideogram for the rest of my life.

✶

Burning to Know

When an industry dies: there will always be someone to cherish its cooling embers. The American Accordion Musicological Society "has established a museum of antique accordions" in Pitman, New Jersey. The Center for the History of Foot Care and Foot Wear, in Philadelphia: seven hundred shoes, from a pair of Egyptian burial sandals circa 2000 B.C., to the fetishy pumps and mules of Hollywood hotshots.

Phillumenists, "lovers of light": collectors of matchbooks. Some have—believe me—in excess of a million. Introduced in 1894, the promotional matchbook has, in the century since, become the zillioned, overmuch, slip-in-a-pocket canvas on which we've pictured the face of our national life in all of its grandeur and tawdriness: the sunstruck jetting spire of Old Faithful; a domino-fall of sliced Spam.

The ones I like best, of these remnant squares and oblongs from a quickly obsolescing world of prideful public smoking, are the ones that show yet other dead or endangered subjects: doubling the minor-key wistfulness. A vegetable pushcart ("Get 'Em Fresh!"). Hats, both men's and women's, in their lavishly substantial "hat boxes," because the right chapeau deserves its own luggage. The Chili Bowl Restaurant (featuring "Barbu-cated Steaks"): shaped to its name exactly. A truly beautiful matchbook, wherein every individual match is printed to look like a fountain pen. And here's a happy pinup cutie (doubling) in her gartered nylons (tripling) at a manual typewriter (fully *quadrupling* the wistful thrill of contemplating ambiences in dwindlement): she's "Just My Type!" Maybe she'll contact Dixie Evans, President of the Exotic Dancers League of America (Helendale, California, off Route 66): "The League collects photographs, playbills, costumes, and other memorabilia of this rousing and original American tradition."

"I used to keep my matchbooks in a brandy snifter. Now I have *four hundred* brandy snifters."

They meet once a year. They internet. They publish their various newsletters.

"Every wall of my house is completely covered."

How do they do it?—the usual passion.

Why do they do it?—one group calls itself Keepers of the Flame.

I imagine it this way: running/sneaking/running at dusk, when everyone else is inside eating or clustered around the flickering interplanetary-blue of the TV screen in expectation of *I Love Lucy* or the show that scooted Lucy out of the coveted number-one spot in 1956, *The $64,000 Question*.

Running—madly. And maybe catching himself at isolated moments, slowing, strolling nonchalantly—mad, but smart. His silver-starred silk scarf imported from Genoa gets snagged on an alley catalpa's dangling claw. He leaves it, he doesn't even notice it—careless. But hearing the blood thumpthumpthump in his temples to the beat of some triumphant Old World martial air. The book of matches is in his jacket pocket, and I imagine it's one of their own, that he saved: "Best Cases ACCORDING To Everyone!" They thought this motto was clever.

We'll never know his motive. The insurance money? But that was so diddly a walletful. I believe it was more in the way of a vast incendiary cleansing, and the swan-song glory of seeing that horrible tiger lily of fire snap and fold against the black night sky. I imagine him standing there, doing an in-place series of those same emphatic stomps I saw at the funeral. Leaping—and sobbing, I imagine.

They soon enough caught him, of course. As if he weren't a primo suspect anyway, there was that evidential scarf. I imagine that *he* imagined a scarf of smoke around his neck, as they hustled him into the cop car. First, he'd try to wear it with dignity: who were *they* to determine *his* actions! Then, by stages, it must have sunk in: a vagrant had died. She'd been huddled up rotgut-blotto in a side door all the while. They made him look at her reeking remains: one held his head above the body, and the other forcibly opened his eyes, and kept them wide for minutes.

The rest I can't imagine: it gibbers away across a border beyond my introspection. I only know that the other inmates call him The Legend—a third, a final, El—and that (to do him some justice) feeling even a useless guilt like his, implies a moral component.

I wish I could write about this today. I wish that . . . If I *had* an understanding of the foreign moral conduct of an A-security ward, then maybe I could *start* to start to understand the next thing, Dog Bone Hill, which seems to me to be a world without a moral component altogether. Maybe it's there, and my xenophobic First World eyes are blind to its grace and its dignity. Or maybe it *isn't* there, not now, not yet, not in the middle of the backbreak, weevily day, when every calorie of human expression beyond an occasional grunting fuck is needed simply for climbing out of the rubble and crawling back in it by night.

And at Dog Bone Hill, and at Paradise Hole, and at Little Cry, the death squads own the town, if "town" is the word for sheet tin shacks, if "squad" is the word for seeing one's own country-men in masks, with pig-eviscerating knives, and in their bellies a scream that could power the wheels of Monte Carlo for centuries.

Even now, they're destroying something—but I'm no primary voice for that. Even now, they're beating away the carrion birds and rebuilding—but I can't speak for this. The future is theirs, as the cities decay, and the cultures clash, and the resources yield and scale off. The future is theirs, and the past is dead, there is no past, just a daily barbaric beginning—and there is no looking back and no nostalgia without a tended-to past.

Even now, they're lined up on the edge of an encampment, hun-gry, keening, cursing, lifting pitchforks, calling down lightning to crawl their scalps—tinder awaiting igniting.

I can't represent this new world. I can only trust that, nonetheless, my small pique means that somewhere else is the flame of an eloquent outrage, and my fondness means that somewhere else a burning longing roars inside a heart.

Swiss Warblers. Echoes.

Now nobody smokes—the unregenerate smoke, the last Cro-Magnon and untutored among us, only those. We know now, tiparillo smoke will coil in a lung like an anaconda, a wreath of it lingers there as if nailed to a blackened shanty wall.

And yet I can't shrug off the beauties of that earlier mode, and who could more objectively delineate their praise than I, non-smoker always (nary a one), as if a collateral member of the family were called on, for the eulogy.

The lighters in every engineered fantasia, Lucite flame-thrower dragons, gold-plated sputniks, palm trees, penguins. Humidors of cedarwood and ivory inlay, scrimshawed over with lotus-bordered scenes of pharaonic splendor or, more familiarly, Scottie dogs. An automaton, from France in the 1940s, features a hookah-using pasha, feathered, bejeweled, and turbaned, who puffs out blooms of smoke (from a cigarette you insert) and then clears the air with a wave of his peacock fan. On the other hand, the boomerang swoops of certain deco ashtrays stun the eye by their very severity.

Mainly I remember (from observing, not from practicing) the semiotics of cigarettes, their way of physically making exclamation points, and bridge-like raisings or lowerings of esteem, and italicized passions, appear in the air. I remember clearly seeing faintheartedness steel itself in the swagger loaned by a smoke—and seeing, too, smoke soften the brunt of a loneliness. My parents smoked: two heads in a mutual nimbus. There have been times (a diner counter in rural Pennsylvania at 4 A.M., a frowzy downtown Greyhound Bus lounge made a ragtag Noah's Ark by hammerpounding downpour . . .) when I've seen that smoke as the tapestry fabric keeping otherwise fly-apart lives in a pattern, when I've seen that omni-contributed haze as the by-products smoke of democracy at work. An esperanto.

Once, I asked a friend why he smoked. He gave the answer I think my father would have provided if I'd asked him, if we'd talked that kind of talk.

I imagine it this way:

He was known as someone to call if a building caught fire.

Back then, what seemed to be a containable blaze was often fought by one official pumper truck and a corps of reliable amateurs from the neighborhood. (It was seen as a neighborhood entertainment, too—a form of open-air Grand Guignol. Thus has it ever been.) How far was he still from the clamor, when he recognized the building as his brother-in-law's, the failed and partially boarded-up Two-Els?

Well, they'd save 80 percent for the wreckers to have a swing at, a week or two later. Not a major blaze by any means. But that's pure retroknowledge; at the panicky, hell-tinged moment, it was touch-and-go ferocity enough for anybody's pulse.

Earlier I compared the flames to a tiger lily, but that was wrong. More of a lion, wildly maned. More of an inferno of a rose, its billowing petals of lethal saffron and henna, its charry attar.

That's not it either. That's writer-speech. It's fourteen men saying *shit* and O *Jesus* in front of that monstrous Fahrenheit heart. He took his orders, he smashed his share of windows open, he felt the invisible sear along his skin, and the pulmonary danger entering his throat. And then it was over, somehow. Out of the chaos, they'd brought it under control.

As always, a few of the neighbors provided coffee and donuts from their own kitchen tables. Some wives and girlfriends appeared, with their usual tearful ministrations, and the rough jokes in return. For the most part, everyone motionless, awed by what had happened and by their escape from it—*this* time. Everyone feeling the cool, ensuing blackness of the night like a balm, like a sleep mask over the whole spent body. Then someone shared her pack of smokes: tribal. Tiny orange points of constellated glow against the intricate, ravenous universe. That was almost all you could see: those dots of community.

Then, by ones and twos, they drifted off. I imagine we could stand in place and watch, and follow him home that way, as he walked those couple of midnight miles. Soon, we'd only know him by the dance of that breath-fed firefly—that feeble but familiar lantern leading him back to a place of human lives in proper balance. We could watch him, that way, disappear into the dark of forty years ago. Eventually we'll every one of us enter that darkness. For now, though, we dasn't.

Whitman's America

Sheila says Sandy's scheduled to be transferred to Chicago for a year and she's going too, with the baby. "Now that the marriage is finally getting stronger, I don't want to take a risk."

"That's good," I tell her. "You know, it reminds me of Cousin Elmer and Cousin Ettie—" but Sheila is *on a roll.*

And Sheila says that Sandy's older son, from his first (shit) marriage, "except they weren't *really, legally* married," is certainly not a part of this sudden, mandated year away, "but of course he could visit on weekends." And Sheila says her therapist has switched her from Prozac to Paxil—and with the latter, there's the bonus of weight loss as well.

"Sometimes I think I'm the only person in town who isn't on . . ."

"Oh Goldbarth, hush. Do you know why everyone's so depressed? There are too many choices. Once upon a time you had a home, your people, a piece of land or a job, and maybe all of it was limiting, but you weren't torn in eighty thousand possible directions like now. The brain hasn't caught up with eighty thousand possible directions."

"Is that how *you* feel?"

"*Now,* a life is something that picks you apart. It's not like in that Whitman poem you taught us, where his life held him in place, his life was like the universe and it held him in place. (Did I get it right?)"

✦

He called himself "a kosmos." The term had been popularized not long before by Alexander von Humboldt, the Prussian naturalist whose *Cosmos: A Sketch of a Physical Description of the Universe* attempts not only to list, but to link in a meaningful pattern, "all that we know . . . of heaven and earth, from the nebulae of the stars to the geography of mosses."

It was a "harmony, or blending together of all created things," that lit the omnivorous vision of Humboldt, and it was comfortingly anthropocentric; Whitman writes that "Humboldt, in his Kosmos, citing Schiller, has observed of the Greeks: 'With them the landscape is always the mere background of a picture, in the foreground of which human figures are moving.'"

Cosmos of course *is* Greek: the protoprinciple counterbalance to *Chaos*. And so it means "order" and "unity" and, by easy extension, "everything"—if you think that order and unity *are* attributes of everything.

They were for Whitman. *Kosmos* is defined in his notebook as "noun masculine or feminine, a person who[se] scope of mind . . . includes all, the whole known universe." The key here is *known;* for Whitman, standing there bardically in a world still antecedent to the everhammering info-wham of atomsmasher physics, and cyberinfinity, and the fizzle of the family unit, and blah blah blah . . . it was possible—okay, barely; okay, wishfully; but *possible*—to posit that the limits of Creation, and the range of its motley inventory, could be *known.*

From his country's multi-tumult, from its blackwhite-richpoor-northsouth-manifestdestinyness in action, Whitman fashions what he calls "a race"—not a nation; a race, as if the thousand American differences could truly, on the ground of his imagination, be subsumed at last into a great and seamless entity.

"I contain multitudes," says Whitman. In "The Sleepers" he

isn't content to emphatically imagine sleeping bodies by the billions on a given night, not Whitman:

> I dream in my dream all of the dreams of the other dreamers
> And *I become* the other dreamers. (my emphasis)

This great gesture symbolizes the comforting world of that accommodation Sheila yearns for, and so do I and so do you, we see it by a softening humanist glow that's settled along the various clearly labeled levels of the earlier, more linear, and still-so-very-appealing Great Chain of Being.

Maybe I'm kidding myself about the really hands-on viability of feeling this sort of belongingness, this encompassingness, in 1860. Whitman had seen the nation unstitch; he knew what that economic and philosophical schism meant to a sixteen-year-old trumpeter offering a burst, gangrenous leg to the farmyard saw of the amputation man in a ward at the close of the War. He wasn't blind to the everyday life of drunkards, strumpets, all of the lost and vibrant pennygrubbing street life at the bottom of his country's stratification. The flux of his own, primarily unacknowledged sexuality surely was a torment.

So maybe even in 1860 his artistic mission required a carefully monitored ignorance. *Leaves of Grass* had gone through six editions, with three more still to come in Whitman's life, when Albert Einstein was born in 1879. It was a threshold world, a peephole-to-the-future world, with just one breath of human time before the first studies in astral spectroanalysis would bear fruit. And we know from his poem "When I Heard the Learn'd Astronomer" that Whitman once stomped out in disgust (he says; was it fear?) from an astronomy lecture.

It could be he intuited what was coming, all of the iffy indeterminacy and overload of Sheila's life at half-past-noon in August 1996 . . . and chose to retreat to his own well-shaped, self-regulatory system. I'm *not* trying to paint Walt Whitman (who "believe[d] in Darwinianism and evolution from A to izzard") as any reactionary thinker. But for all of the discord allowed in his poems, everyone has an apportioned role, and a rightness—the politician, the dignified Indian squaw, the bosun's mate, the blacksmith—and so do the grasses, and the dungpile beetles, and so do the suns.

And although it's true that Stephen Hawking's search is for a Unifying Theory that makes soulmates of the "strong" and "weak" nuclear forces *and* the electromagnetic force *and* gravitation *and* time, group-wedding them into one cohesive, elegant, supraexplanatory formula in the same way Humboldt attempted to incorporate both the spirals of the galaxies and the spirals of fiddlehead ferns into a single governing field . . . nonetheless, perception is all; we see the cosmos of the twentieth century birthed in unimaginable explosion, and its afterthought *Homo sapiens* citizens born of a meiotic division that haunts them in one hundred different pull-apart ways for the length of their stay on this planet.

For Humboldt—still believing in his nineteenth-century version of this Unity—time is the even reeling-out of a plot with human protagonists. For Hawking, time is so ultimately distortable . . . he's even come to look like one of those puddled watches in Dali paintings. And *then?* "I don't know *anyone* who feels anchored"—what Sheila says.

When I think of what Sheila says, I think of a photograph from the last days of the Civil War. I can't tell if the air is actually smoky or if the fixative has thickened; in either case, the scene is horribly clear. A child has died, and a mother is lifting its shoebox-size pine coffin, with a grievous, broken gesture, to her ear, as if for a final communication. And then I see one of my friends, with a cellular phone, in the same pose, also hopelessly looking for contact—talking, waiting for an answer from nowhere, stumbling with this useless receiver into a swale of gathering clouds that are seeded with nothing but personal woe, *hello? hello?* forever.

✦

It reminds me of Cousin Elmer and Cousin Ettie. I mean the mention of war, and the imagery of aimlessness; I mean the fear that Sheila has of a leave-taking breaking her marriage.

That's what happened: he was called to the European front not six months after the honeymoon. Ettie tells me, "That night we went dancing. It was going to be our last night together for who-knew-*how*-long." She's seventy-nine. When she tells a story, her hands move in her lap as if she's fashioning tiny figures of her characters three-dimensionally from clay, in secret. Trying to envision that motion fifty-five years back now—squinting into time, against its flow—I can see the attractive girlishness, the modest sense of personal style, that had (as my mother put it) all the boys like bees around a rose. That flower is liverspotted now, but not without some remnant of its gender-chemistry power.

"He *loved* to dance, we both did. Do you know the rhumba? I *think* it was the rhumba. And he would throw all of his weight on his right leg, he was *very* strong, and lift me, and twirl me around in his arms like a pinwheel. Everyone would stop their own dance, just to watch . . ." And then the dreaminess gets clouded. "But you know, little things, a *nothing,* and words get said. That night, we said some of those words. He thought I was flirting with . . . anyway, the point is, *you* were divorced once, Albert, *you* know." Yes I do, allrighty, indeed I remember those army ants in their march through the maze of the brain.

"And then he left the next day. We didn't say a goodbye, no hug, no nothing, he was a frown and a rucksack, and then he was gone. His stupid pride!—he didn't write no letters, *I* didn't write." She gives a light smack to her forehead with the heel of one hand: "My stupid *khop.*"

"What then?"

"It was like we were having a fight, but without the satisfaction of fighting. I didn't know from *what* he was doing Over There. For me, I walked around like drunk, in a daze, I did things that . . . I didn't care about anything, I'd speak to strangers, some of them weren't so good for me if you want to know the truth. They were very bad times . . . I don't want to talk about it." Her hands are shredding the air in her lap.

They were *very* bad times, and Cousin Ettie's story, "if you want to know the truth," can't even *start* to jiggle the needle on the grief-o-meter. My own much-coddled intimations of what the world was like in the 1940s would have included the War-era comic books that I'd inherit, tattered but intact, a decade after their date of issue.

They had *furious* graphics. The covers of *All Select, All Winners,* and *Marvel Mystery Comics* show The Human Torch (a kind of flying body on total fire) and The Sub-Mariner (the deepsea-breathing Prince of Atlantis; and please, it's *máriner,* not *maríner*) teamed in busily dizzying scenarios, battling the Axis powers. On dozens of covers, the angry-browed Sub-Mariner overturns a German warship, shaking its occupants into the briny deep like so much vermin wildly tumbling out from an infested couch. On *Marvel Mystery* No. 16, The Human Torch, swooping a beautiful aerial parabolic arc across the cover, combusts a Nazi-stronghold oil tank with the touch of his thermal body.

No holds, as they say, were barred. "The Nazi scum" were often so barbaric, they'd devolved in evolution: an endless series of those swastika-emblazoned troops were fanged and slavering, taloned, bat-eared devils. "The Japs" were so bucktoothed that some of them look as if they're mouthing a splayed deck of cards. I might be embarrassed now to cackle over the wild energy of this art in front of my German and Japanese friends. But back then . . . it was war, after all. And after all, we'd been attacked.

And it must have been wonderful, in a way, for a boy with all of his hormonal burbling building up under the skin, to have this enemy—this outlet—that was sanctioned by the culture-at-large. It's often sports. Later, it would be communists. In the summer of 1943 it happened to be an ickily evil samurai-looking fellow, who was threatening a bound American redheaded lass with his ritual sword: The Human Torch punches his arm and the flesh of his bicep melts like a gory wax.

It was wonderful, too, to have The Torch and Subby "fighting side by side!!!" as *Marvel Mystery* No. 15 ballyhooed. As recently as No. 9, they'd been frantically whacking away (I mean with ripped-out midtown skyscraper I-beams) at *one another,* seeking each other out for this with the grim fanaticism you'd expect from such an elemental antagonism: fire and water. They couldn't be at peace and yet they couldn't be apart, and in their own thin way they surely stood for all of the ancient dueling units: medulla oblongata and neocortex; God and no-God; man and woman; Elmer and Ettie . . .

In fact, their rivalrous banter accrues the feel of bickering, of snippiness, we associate with the way that lovers put pet names to sneer-lipped, quarrelsome use. For a poem, I once compiled a catalog from one of their many sparrings: "You flaming fool!" "You water rat!" "This is the end of you, my little glo-worm!" "Here! I've got you at last, my fine water-moccasin!" "Fire-bug!" "Water-bug!" It may as well be marriage counseling.

We might say the War effort wedded them—they had a common cause, and made for a powerful pair. And that was true of most of the country: scrap drives, GI mail drives, coupon rationing, cadres of amateur nurses' aides, a nation unified under a single vast wave of volunteerism.

How different from my memories of the home front during the Viet Nam years! The fractured needs. The partisan harangues. The hate. In comic book terms, it wasn't simply a matter of Fire

Superhero and Water Superhero squaring off. It seemed—I was twenty, and tender, and stuffed with ire and angst—that *every* element imaginable had given rise to a supercharacter. Argon Man, Uranium Woman, Linoleum Girl, The Mink Oil Kid, Black Powermonger, Good Ole White Boy, Screech-Owl Woman, The Hawk, The Dove, The Invisible Neutrino, The Plague . . . were duking it out in the crowded, superflown-through air, and pulling apart the psyche of two American generations, into what Sheila calls, despondently, the eighty thousand directions.

Some time last summer I drove to Burns, a one-light Kansas town about fifty-five minutes out of Wichita. Tim Burton's crew from Hollywood was here, to shoot their scenes of wheatfield ambience for *Mars Attacks*. The dream boys in their jeans-ad ponytails, and the titty- and nose-ring script girls, mingled successfully with the gingham daughters of church-going Burns, and its kitchen-bowl-haircut sons, and everyone buying into the fiction that the Other, the Cancer, the Foreigner, wasn't someone sipping coffee two booths down in the lone café, but was of extraterrestrial origin, overtly coneheaded, tentacled, and creepily oviparous.

We require a foe that we can fear together—that we can fear, and so hate, and so pummel into bloody wads together. Shrewdly recognizing this, the mavens of popular culture have given us outer space aliens this season: green blood. Nothing could work neater. We will cleanse ourselves in xenophobic rage against these raygun-toting slimies, and never risk the kind of internal rupture we suffer from in something like "the war on drugs": one organ of the national body ostracizing brother organs.

Much of the sorrow the country experienced during the Civil War was due, beyond the surface carnage, to a sense of internal sundering: we had made *ourselves* the enemy, like some mad beast trying to gnaw itself in two. The theme of "brother versus

brother" becomes a Civil War cliché, and has its basis in the real
tears shed in real American households.

Not that the monstrous surface carnage wasn't grief enough.
"610,000 dead," is the figure David S. Reynolds provides, "and
425,000 with debilitating wounds." In his notebooks Whitman
says that "future years will never know the seething hell and the
black infernal background of countless minor scenes and interiors." And "Andersonville, Salisbury, Belle-Isle, &c., (not Dante's
pictured hell and all of its woes, degradations, filthy torments,
excell'd those prisons)." In his three years as an unofficial cotside
nurse, he visited up to 100,000 soldiers, offering jellies, candies,
stationery, apples, tobacco, writing their letters, listening, holding
hands. "Out doors, at the foot of a tree, I notice a heap of ampu-
tated feet, legs, arms, hands, &c., a full load for a one-horse cart."

Even this enormity fit inside his Humboldt-like vision of a
wholeness. Life is not "chaos—it is form, union, plan" . . . and
the proper healer, shaman-like, can help reverse the loss of these,
in the physical being, as well as in the social order. (To this extent,
his *Leaves of Grass* can be seen as a cotside visit to an ailing culture—a poet's textual laying-on of hands.)

The early poems exhorting the riled-up of America to enlist
"avoided partisanship, picturing the war spirit as a unifying rather
than divisive force" (Reynolds). Even his notebooks' mournful-
ness is unsided: ". . . the dead, the dead, the dead—*our* dead . . .
South or North, ours all (all, all, all, finally dear to me)." And at
the War's close, he's eager to begin a notebook entry with this:
"I restore my book to [a] bracing and buoyant equilibrium." Balance. Kosmos. Sketches from nature.

Of all of his work, "The Sleepers"—202 lines—seems to me
especially vivid in its presentation of physical and psychic renewal. Wrapped like corpses (yes, but also like fetuses) in the all-
democratizing deeps of the night, a catalogued cast of Whitmanic
variety (but heavy on the unfortunates)—the maimed, the feeble-

minded, the disconsolately lonely, "the midnight widow," "the consumptive," and the rest—come under the poet's own transfiguring imagination:

> I swear they are averaged now—one is no better than the other,
> The night and sleep have likened them and restored them.
>
> . . . the exile returns home,
> The fugitive returns unharmed—the immigrant is back beyond
>   months and years,
> . . .
> The Dutchman voyages home, and the Scotchman and Welshman
>   voyage home, and the native of the Mediterranean voyages
>   home,
> To every port of England and France and Spain enter well-filled
>   ships,
> The Swiss foots it toward his hills—the Prussian goes his way, and
>   the Hungarian his way, and the Pole goes his way,
> The Swede returns, and the Dane and Norwegian return
> . . .
> The Asiatic and African are hand in hand—
> . . .
> Stiflings and passages open—the paralysed become supple
> . . .
> They pass the invigoration of the night and the chemistry of the
>   night and awake.

And as I remember these lines . . .

"Wake up already, Mr. War Hero. We're *talking* about you." Elmer wakes up. He's probably slept this way through fully half of Ettie's stories for the last two decades. "Listen to yourself some time," he says, "and see if *you* stay awake."

"You came home when?" I ask him.

"*What* 'when'?"

"From Europe, from the War."

"Oh, maybe a month after this." He lifts his stump—the right leg ends halfway to where the knee once was—and swivels it a bit, as if to start a spangled hoop in action for some circus act.

Then he looks across to Ettie for confirmation of his hazy calendrical sense.

"Yes, say a month, a month and a week. That's when"—she turns to me, to continue her tale—"the army sends me a letter. Not Elmer, the *shtoonk* . . ."

"Yeah, so? Like *you* wrote *me,* the whole time I was crawling on my belly through *dreck,* Miss Smarty?"

". . . I bought a ticket, and I visited him in the hospital, I see this amputation . . ."

"What can I say? Back then they didn't give you no superduper pathetic legs . . ."

"Pros-thet-ic." She corrects him with a finicky overpronunciation. This is love, in a language individuated for fifty-five years.

"So anyway, I see this amputation, and I think, you know, how frail we are, and loss, and . . ."

"Oy. With the weeping now." He rolls his eyes.

". . . and suddenly I'm sitting in the bed by him, and we're hugging."

"This is good advice," he tells me. "Hug."

Tonight, this two-bit imprecation circles around in the back of my brain, appreciating in value with every revolution. I look in, at my wife asleep, and I hear it. I read the front page of the paper—all of the chosen animosities, misjudgments, and deceptions from the preceding twenty-four hours—and I hear it. "Hug." The word's been so demeaned by touchy-feely healy-therapy groups . . . I look in again at my wife, I think of my ex-wife, "I wander all night in my vision . . . I go from bedside to bedside." Is it possible he can redeem that word?

I wanted this to be a wish, a farewell valedictory, for Sheila; but I see it's a wish for everybody I'm fond of. I don't care if it's simplistic, I don't even care if you claim that I'm misreading him, or claim that he misread the map of the human heart as it unfurled under his gaze, I want Walt Whitman's implicit *Rx* for America: reconciliation.

To Write of Repeated Patterns

They say he's sixteen. They say in the dead of the night—they really *do* say this, "the dead of the night"—he sneaks to the attic, planned or unplanned nobody yet knows, he lifts his daddy's "squirrel gun" from its case, then sneaks back down with it, carefully opens the door to the room in which they're sleeping, and blasts them out of this life, one shot to the temple each, in quick succession. The neighbors are interviewed, ". . . shocked" ". . . a *wonderful* boy" ". . . he *loved* his parents." Then the camera brings him into its painfully clear-edged imagery. He's seated behind a desk at headquarters, confused by himself, by everything and everyone. He doesn't look over twelve, a limp rag doll of a child, being questioned for parricide.

Skyler and I are at Sarah's and Eric's. "Change the channel!" What we'd wanted was mild diversion floating in over our afternoon beers. There's TV snow and lightning bolts; then, a couple of numbers up or down the dial, the news is into its loonier wrap-up phase: "There was three of them, three feet high. They was green." A trucker spotted them trotting down a playground-slideish gangplank "from a silver ship. It looked like, you know . . ." ". . . a shark's fin fitted with lateral wings," the one other observer, a priest, chimes in. A *priest?* "They peered around, returned to the ship, and took off. That's all. I think they were trying to bring us a *message.*"

Tonight, while Skyler's asnooze, I'm up with a book. It says, in the voice of classical lamentation, "A man looks on his own son as his enemy. The heart is aggressive, blood is everywhere, no office functions properly. The rich wake poor, the poor wake rich, the land whirls around like a potter's wheel." Verily. The television yea-sayeth this with every snoopy camcorder shot of a presidential rally or a weekend convention of skateboard and dirtbike enthusiasts. Some group of PTA sex education fanatics, costumed à la birds and bees. Some show of support for a local pastor in jail on charges of fondling a ten-year-old girl. The remains of an airliner: yes, a three-member suicide squadron smuggled a plastic gun on board in six unrecognizable segments. "Everywhere men are killed wrongfully."

This text, however, is from the Egyptian Old Kingdom— 2500 B.C. Some nights—this isn't the first time I've consulted it after overmuch media brouhaha—its cannily contempo applicability leaves me shaking. My head in a bleary wonder, blinking my eyes not so much at a world gone mad (which would, at least, be an adventure) but a world that's always been, and is continually, mad.

I may as well also admit that Skyler and I have squabbled. I'm downstairs reading inside an invisible bubble of self-righteousness. She's upstairs in bed, and emanating waves of anger out of her body, regular convection currents the instruments would pick up as scarlets and indigos. We'll make up soon—tomorrow, most likely. We'll add our latest display of this commonest syndrome to its history. We've done it before, the billions before us have done it before, the tiffing couples on pleasure barges beached along the Nile have had their ritual version of skirmish-and-smooch, and some nights when I finally tamp myself under the sheets beside her, I see we're two strokes of an all-over pattern repeated—past where sight thins out—across the fabric of being human, or being alive at all.

⁺⁺

If I'm going to write of repeated patterns, let me mention the relatively well-known mid-twelfth-century report of William of Newburgh, about "an unheard-of prodigy, which took place during the reign of King Stephen." Incredible though its details are, he "was so overwhelmed by the weight of so many and such competent witnesses" that he feels, finally, "no regret at having recorded an event so miraculous."

By a village of East Anglia, at harvest time, two children emerged from "some very ancient cavities" near the fields, where the reapers found them wandering in a daze—"a boy and a girl, completely green in their persons, and clad in garments of a strange colour, and unknown materials."

They couldn't speak English; for months they ate only raw beans from the pod, "until they learned the use of bread. At length, by degrees, they changed their original colour, through the natural effect of our food, and became like ourselves." (*Reader, let a bell go off.*)

Then they told a story of having been whisked here from "the land of St. Martin" where the sun doesn't rise, and all is perpetual twilight, but the countryfolk are Christian. They were tending their father's flocks when they both "heard a great sound . . . we became on a sudden entranced, and found ourselves among you in the fields."

The boy died not long after. His sister "continued in good health" and "was married at Lynne, and was living a few years since."

This isn't the earliest sighting of green otherpeople by any means, but something in its narrative and phrasing gives it the first truly modern cachet. It's tempting to think of it as the patriarch-story (siblingarch-story, really) from which an anecdotal family of wunderkinder and aliens descend, yet it's more properly just one very fine retelling in a line of tellings immeasurably long.

Eight hundred years away from William of Newburgh, I pick up one of those supermarket tabloids devoted to cheap astonishment. June 12, 1990: MOM ON VEGGIE DIET GIVES BIRTH TO GREEN BABY. "'Even the whites of his eyes are pale green,' notes stunned Dr. Dominic Valenso." He's the cover story, staring out at me cute and gooing. He's printed in no inconclusive hint of light lime, but a deep and even Saint-Paddy's-Day-green inked freely from a tube that's labeled *Shamrock*. "'It'll take some time, but with a well-balanced diet the baby should lose the green color eventually,' Dr. Valenso promises." (*Reader, does this ring a bell?*) Meanwhile, "teary-eyed mom Consuela Alvarez" wrings her lovely cocoa-colored Caucasian hands.

✦

I've zeroed it down to that handful of seconds of TV sputter while Sarah was switching channels. Before that, everything was copacetic. Right after, Skyler started with those only-Albert-can-recognize-them petulant glances that—well, but she'd have another version. I brought up subject x or y; I cranked on into my supercilious mode, with that look I beam out by tilting my head down and glaring *over* the rims of my glasses . . .

The truth is, neither one of us has a clue as to why we've suddenly lowered the interpersonal temperature of our house to that of a meatlocker. There's no issue being battled. Ideas of right and wrong aren't at stake. We only know we brought a sliver of coolness home from Sarah's and Eric's, and managed to fan the thing—a snideness here, a willful misinterpretation there—into a big berg.

This "isn't like us." We're normally sweet in our love, and sane. In a truce of a few talky minutes' duration before bed, Skyler says, "I think we've been taken over by outerspace beings. I can feel it. They're growing some gunk in our heads. Seeds." She's really *into* it now. "If our heads were sliced open they'd look like cantaloupes: all those alien seeds in the center."

So that's when it happened, I'm theorizing: the TV fizz was an interdimensional portal, through which the little green creatures from Planet Unimaginable grabbed hold of our unwary minds. That way, the two of us aren't at fault. That way, external agency as large as science fiction bears the blame.

And I mean it, too, if by the formulation "little green creatures" I get to mean our reptilian selves, which were there in the primal underdrift of our brains before our brains were even undifferentiated plasm laboring toward shape—our gilled and serpent-tailed lizard selves, our circulating of cold blood through the rockbottom saurian folds.

What I'd like to do now is remind you of some fourteenth-century narrative goings-on. The scene is Christmastide at Camelot, and at the Round Table *with all the meat and the mirth that men could devise* are Arthur, *the comeliest king,* and his courtly followers, *the most noble knights known under Christ, and the loveliest ladies that lived on earth ever.* All is ceremonially festive. Their initial course is served, to the accompaniment of trumpets, drums, and *noble pipes,* and all of the world seems good and in order to these good, orderly personages, but—*scarce were the sweet strains still in the hall* when *there hurtles in at the hall door an unknown rider.* Larry D. Benson says, "The action is suddenly suspended, and over ninety lines are devoted to a carefully detailed portrait."

Put simply, the man is *oureal enker grene,* entirely green. His lavish beard is green. His *raiment noble* is green; the ermine mantle, the hood, the hose, the spurs, the belt and its bosses, the saddle—*all his vesture verily [is] verdant green,* and he rides *a green horse great and thick.* A tang of wildness radiates like green aurora borealis, emerald, celadon, flickering poplar. Something hugely out of the ordinary is glowering over the roast.

There hurtles in at the hall-door . . . In the still of this civilized gathering, it must be as if an interdimensional portal—*zzzt!*—has opened wide.

By its own Middle English audience, the aspect of the Green Knight in *Sir Gawain and the Green Knight*—or the facets of his aspect—would have been easily read. A literary figure himself, he incorporates stock folk-art figures that trail back, by ballad and creaking tavern sign, to some preliterate origin lost in green fog.

The "green man" is a "wild man"—Benson says "in folk ritual they are interchangeable." Here, at the court of Arthur, the clues are clanked onstage: the intruder is rude in speech and in action, he brandishes an axe, his look is savage, and it culminates in that formidable beard, as *big as a bush on his breast,* the poet says, referring us to the color again. And Benson: "In medieval art the wild man often wears both hair and leaves." He is stern, perhaps hostile, and "the enemy of the knight and the opponent of the values represented by the romance courts."

At the same time, the figure in green is Youth (I was a freshman, green at the game myself, when I first encountered the poem) and, not surprisingly, Nature in benign guise. In *The Parlement of the Thre Ages*, Youth is *gerede alle in grene.* "One finds the same green-clad figure throughout fourteenth-century literature"— vital, sweet to look upon, laughing musically into the breeze— and, by uncomplicated association, the figure comes to be symbolic of love, of springtime foliage, finally of Life itself. In the fourteenth-century work *Le Songe vert,* the narrator contemplates suicide, swoons, but then is revived by Venus and her attendants and clothed by them *entire de vert.* In *Death and Life* the latter figure is *comlye clad in kirtle and mantle of goodliest greene that euer groome ware.*

If you subscribe to a full year of a supermarket tabloid, it's those same opposing twins you'll meet in alternate issues, repeatedly: the evil aliens bent on enslavement, nabbing up late-night drivers from behind the wheel, strapping them onto the tables of weirdly wired Martian-scientific surgery; and the aliens of light, of peace (I think of the dove descending with the green sprig in its beak); they bring advice, and hope; they bear the shoots of other, older worlds, by which a new green Eden will blossom for us in our soil and in our hearts.

We can follow these figures through time along unbroken vines, the figures themselves now tuber-like, below our daily notice, and now bunched up in splashy clumps.

It seems unquestionable that the wild man, the representor of everything feral lurking inside green shadow (or: in am/bush), is a presence of unfathomably ancient creation. Cain, the farmer and fratricide, is his ancestor. So is Enkidu the beast-man, foe at first and then the blood brother of King Gilgamesh: we see him on cylinder seals battling lions no more lushly maned than he is, and often this battle is formulaically rendered to look more like the ballroom whorl of happy partners. How far back does he go, this figure? How far back do our psyches extend?

As a character with a number of type associations, the wild man "survived among the peasantry of continental Europe well into the nineteenth century" (Benson), and a study titled *Homo Sapiens Ferus* (1888) reports "A girl of nine or ten years entered the village of Songy at dusk. Her feet were naked, her body was covered with rags and skins of animals. She wore a piece of bottle-gourd on her head. She carried a club in her hand, and when someone in the village set a dog at her she gave it such a heavy blow on the head that the animal fell over dead at her feet." The threatening pod people lurching amok in s-f movies are cousins to her, the scaly and often antenna'ed creatures that stalk the streets of our fairest cities, the green blob/slime that carries whole groups of supporting actors and extras out of party scenes in its oozy amoeboid grip.

Likewise, the life-bestowing vegetable god precedes the Green Knight by millennia, but the two are in alliance, leafy link by link. Tammuz, consort of Ishtar and annual bringer of renewal to the Babylonian fields. Osiris, who fertilized Egypt by using his own dismembered body for seeds, who therefore tends to reviving the dead amidst the Sacred Lotus Fields of Eternity. Their largesse, over time, becomes the wealth that's redistributed by a green-outfitted Robin Hood, quartered in his arboreal hold—or Tarzan of the Apes, in whom the law of fang and claw becomes transmuted to the vehicle of our rescue: out of the heavens, out of the thickly bough-canopied heavens, on his magic liana, he'll arc low, lofting us up from our direst moment.

The same green-chapleted face that peers down from the corbeled arch of a thirteenth-century chapel smiles winningly when pushing canned peas and green beans in the Valley of the Jolly (HO-HO-HO) Green Giant (who would later, with the growing kiddie audience in mind, be awarded the youthful sidekick Sprout). It isn't much of a secret that Jung washes clean for us, out of the murk of the ages: "Green is the color of the Holy Ghost, of life, procreation and resurrection."

Frazer, in *The Golden Bough*, details numerous "leaf-clad May Day mummers"—the Leaf King, the Grass King, Jack-in-the-Green . . . Ronald Johnson quotes Lewis Spence: "I have seen him at South Queensferry . . . where he is known as the 'Burry Man,' a boy on whose clothes large numbers of burrs or seed-cases have been so closely sewn that he presents the appearance of a moving mass of vegetation."

In Kenneth Koch's kookily feisty poem "Fresh Air," the stifled spirit of 1950s American poetry—all too hangdog and dyspeptic—is saved from its enemies in the halls of publishing houses and universities by a breath of sexual fervor, intuitive consciousness, and unchained craziness, blowing in over the green of the ocean: "O green, beneath which all of them shall drown!"

✴

Nobody knows what to think. No, make that: *everybody* knows what to think. It simply isn't the same thought.

In the days that follow his being booked on murder charges, Vonnie Coleman, sixteen, is become a cause célèbre, and certain do-good groups are organized in his defense. He's young; his face has a ruggedly puppydog power that attracts, and encourages kindness. There are rumors that the father was in debt to local hoods, and Vonnie became the easy fall guy. His various versions of that night conflict. His so-called confession was hammered together, after all, from the splinters of trauma. Anyway, if he *did* pull the trigger, the rumors say that his parents abused him and photographed it. What about the legal rights of underage suspects? Much media flap.

It doesn't help, however, that his fingerprints are coating the gun. Killing one's parents in sleep takes on a grisliness unnatural even in houses long accommodated to TV reportage of running blood. If the average result of the average roving reporter is to be believed, our average Joe-and-Jane-in-the-street would like to see Vonnie Coleman brought to trial as an adult, and have him sentenced to being eaten alive by rats, an inch or two a day, until only the flesh of his head is with us, begging mercy, and then the rats start at his mouth.

But for my friends and me, the tragedy and its grievous components are part of a picture so large we can't look at Vonnie Coleman except through a historyscope or mythologyscope—and, caught in this focus, he takes his place in a sad continuum sized to the cosmos we live in. He dips sharply out of our consciousness for a couple of hours, then sneakily stitches back in. A day is made of its zillion-and-umpteen stitches, joyous, tormenting, whatever; in the immediate moment, any one of them, half-a-brainwave long, can knock our breath into orbit and drop us to our knees. They're like the stones that make up those "Nazca lines" in Peru—you need to see them from an airplane's height, and *then* there's a chameleon or monkey or star, a meaningful pattern.

At PANDORA'S BOX! EXOTIC DANCERS! I buy a lady called Angel a drink when her set is over. Onstage, she threw sexual heat like an opened furnace. Now, she nearly cowers inside the minimal spandex bands of some chartreuse excuse-of-a-costume. She says, "His face is so innocent. *I* know he didn't do it! And if he did, then we should give him money, you know, government money, and let him start a new life in a different country, don't you think?" I think we should have five minutes of the innocently flirtatious discussion I'd guessed her overpriced drink would buy. But she's heard all the stories, including mine. I know: there are only so many stories.

Later, on my way out, a guy says, "Start by chopping off the sonofabitch's trigger finger. Then his gun hand. Then the arm. I'd like to make my own kid watch that, so he'd learn."

Outside—a patron's left his car lights on, who knows how long? It reminds me, somehow, of Vonnie's face as the cameras always deliver it: his eyes wide open, the rest of him blank, and beams of useless energy I can't understand are burning out into the void.

We've seen this face before: this isn't our first broadcasted pathos. This is Vonnie's face, is Vonnie Coleman's specific face, who could be you or me but for genetic dice in Chance's hands. Yet we can see that this face is cut from a template: the face has preceded the boy, the face will remain when he's only a thimble of elements spilled out, recombining.

Confusion can be useful.

For instance: in the casserole of opposite meanings attached to the Green Knight, Benson finds an intentional "ambiguity [that is] part of the Green Knight's essential character." Merry, then scowling; intruder and, later, host; unappeasable fiend but, in a snap, indulgent friend—"the poet," says Benson, "capitalizes on this ambiguity . . . taking care that his audience remains unsure of whether the green implies good or evil until the very end of the romance."

And what these seemingly conflicting meanings have, at bottom, in common is the Green Knight's utter otherness. As Benson claims, "He comes from another world altogether." Savior or nemesis; citizen of our own psychological shadows or sudden visitor from some "actual" but undiscovered kingdom; nature in all of its howling fury or nature in all of its mysterious verdant nurturing . . . the green is an economy for stating all of these and more, at once—because, no matter the immediate nuance, above all else the Green Knight "always represents a mode of life completely opposed to that represented by [Gawain]."

You betcha. That humongoid presence equestrienned there in the light of the sconces, his skin the color of spinach leaves. Whatever we are, he's else.

In Henry Reed's lyrical novel *The Green Child,* published in 1935, the title character is in many ways a different creature wholly from that figure hulking enormously into Camelot eight hundred years before: a slim defenseless girl, a foundling, she grows up into a slim defenseless woman, with "the same ageless innocent features" informing her countenance now, as in her childhood. Wraithlike. Fey.

Distinctions notwithstanding, though, her lineage is the green warrior's. Her "skin was not white, but a faint green shade, the colour of a duck's egg. It was, moreover, an unusually transparent tegument, and through its pallor the branches spread, not blue and scarlet, but vivid green." And what this betokens, obviously, is someone from an Earth that's not *our* Earth—from "a mode of life completely opposed," as Benson puts it. Reed: "The psychology of the Green Child was a different matter; in a sense, it did not exist."

I say: in a sense it's always existed, parallel to our own, and it will clatter through the castle's staunch portcullis when we least expect.

*

Green can't be more "other" than as elvin-green, the leafy and briery hiding-places of troll and of gnome, often their skin color too (think quick of the witch in *The Wizard of Oz*); when the Green Knight first bursts into Arthur's stronghold, *phantom and faerie the folk there deemed* that startling being.

We're talking pointed ears and impossible laws of physics, we're talking magic rings and chariots drawn by caparisoned mice. In a way, then, the alliance of "green otherness" with fairy lore is its consummate expression.

Or: its consummate expression at a given moment. We live in another moment. This is what Mitchell and Rickard say: "The little people who, by unanimous report, played an intrusive part in daily life up to the Middle Ages, had long been dwindling from their accustomed haunts when suddenly they reappeared, airborne and technologized and up to all their same old tricks. We refer of course to the 'UFO people.' We take this connection seriously. For modern accounts of fairies and the like we must turn to such books as *Flying Saucer Occupants* and *The Unidentified*, where a common phenomenal source for both the fairy and the UFO legend is emphasized."

It's not much more than a matter of adding "atomic propulsion" or "hyper-drive" or "star thrust" into the fairies' forges. Ronald Johnson, describing one more variant of the traditional May Day "green man" figure: "In former times he was also marched in the London Lord Mayor Day's Parade enclosed in a wooden framework on which leaves were clustered and from which came explosions of fireworks." (Picture it landing.) "Chimney sweeps paraded beneath the same pyramidal frameworks on

May Day until the nineteenth century. One imagines them coming like small boxwood topiary, crackling and sparkling through the streets."

(Imagine the "sparkling" stopping, the engine turned off. Imagine them removing their helmets. They venture from the craft. They're saying—what are they saying?—can you make it out?— "Take me to your . . ."—then garble.)

And *their* world, what it's like?—we'll never know. We only have *our* language for it, and that's by definition insufficient. I can give you Dorothy's first view of the Emerald City, however: "The window panes were of green glass; even the sky above the City had a green tint, and the rays of the sun were green. There were many people, men, women and children, walking about, and these were all dressed in green clothes and had greenish skins. At one place a man was selling green lemonade, and when the children bought it Dorothy could see that they paid for it with green pennies."

Here, *she's* the alien. She's come in her frightening flying machine (a standard Kansas farmhouse). " 'What do you wish here in the Emerald City?' 'We came here to see the Great Oz,' said Dorothy." She wants to meet their leader.

Reed's *The Green Child* takes its inspiration from a version of the same folktale William of Newburgh reports—the brother and sister stumbling dazed from the pits, their eating of the beans, the girl's eventual adventures among humankind (in Reed's chosen version, she marries a knight "and was rather loose and wanton in her conduct"). From this green seed his novel flourishes, the children now found wandering in the year 1830, the girl become a water nymph—a naiad—instead of a forest figure: at story's end, she and its human hero sink together "hand in hand . . . below the surface of the pool," those watery recesses being as "other" a realm as the warrens below a fairy knoll.

I first read William of Newburgh's account in John Carey's smart anthology *Eyewitness to History:* seven hundred pages of firsthand reportage that go from plague in ancient Athens to the fleeing of President Marcos from the Philippines in 1982. In his introduction Carey makes the savvy, persuasive case that we can "view reportage as the natural successor to religion."

He reminds us of the constant all-pervadingness of "the media" in our lives; then: "If we ask what took the place of reportage in the ages before it was made available to its millions of consumers, the likeliest answer seems to be religion. Not, of course, that we should assume pre-communication-age man was deeply religious, in the main. There is plenty of evidence to suggest he was not. But religion was the permanent backdrop to his existence"—and, as reportage currently "supplies modern man with a constant and reassuring sense of events going on beyond his immediate horizon" and with "a release from his trivial routines, and a habitual daily illusion of communication with a reality greater than himself," it's easy to see (among many other revealed connections) our tabloidbabble servicing as the way the wonderworking tales of charlatan relic-peddlers must have, once.

If we admit the fairy denizens—the green-girdled, pipes-tootling, impishly tricks-playing Pucks and Pans of the whispered tales—are truly the residua of ancient gods, diminished but refusing to be hooked totally off the psychic stage . . . then we can see our saucermen, yes and Consuela Alvarez's celery-dermis boy-child, as the permutations of raw needs and faint glimmerings of understandings that cycle with steadfast fixity through the surface burble-and-flux of human history.

Skyler and I have "made up"—tonight there's the ritual smooching. All of the details some aspiring short-story writer might observe and scribble into an entry-book—the gooey pet names, the shared reserve of reference-cues that trigger giggling, the hundred knickknack specifics through the room—are ours, are ours alone, and we've toiled long in their compilation. But who would deny the case that our love, as much as our sorrows, reenacts the patterns we're part of, inevitably, from cloverleafs and infinity-signs of submolecular needlepoint, to red-shift, supergalaxy, Big Bang universe swoosh? A flush. A fondle.

Jung relates our deities with our bug-eyed extraterrestrials: "In the threatening situation of the world today, when people are beginning to see that everything is at stake, the projection-creating fantasy soars beyond the realm of earthly organizations and powers into the heavens, into interstellar space, where the rulers of human fate, the gods, once had their abode in the planets."

Reed, with one apt metaphor, connects his water nixie—she of the aqueous depths—with skyscape: at the last, when she returns to her pool after thirty years passed among humans, "her face was transfigured," the narrator tells us, "radiant as an angel's."

✦

But Tasha Coleman, fifteen, doesn't want to hear that the pain in her heart is part of a graphable, overgoverning schema of repetitions. She really does say it that way, "There's a pain," and she points with a wickedly polished but raggedly chewed-at nail, "in my heart." Her face in the TV screen is so very hurt it's barely composed into faceness, and it seems to shimmer in front of us, is more like the reflection of a face, in trembled water.

She had spent the night at a girlfriend's home. She woke up on a different Earth, Earth-X, a world where her parents are dead and her older brother ("I love him still" and she makes another heart-tap) is supposedly their murderer. I don't imagine sleep will ever be the same for her again. Or being awake, for that matter. Do they let her walk through the house? What does she think, approaching that bedroom door? "Think" may not be the word for it; what she *feels,* though, she's said—a pain in her heart. I believe it's a "real," physical excruciation she's talking about, is something like a fishhook stitched beneath the cardiac skin.

And she won't stand your hi-falutin' b.s. or mine about the general shape of pain, and its many guises including the Greek myths blah blah blah. She's had it up to here and we can just go fuck ourselves. The only thing she has in the world right now is that pain, in the back-and-forth threads of nucleic jelly in every cell of Tasha Coleman: that pain. There's no assuagement, but at least she has the knowledge that her pain is monumentally singular, never before such agony and never again, and she doesn't want one syllable that will deprive her of this, so take your chart of literary motifs, shove hard, and waddle on home with your butt clamped tight around it.

Later on, I suspect, she'll turn to one of those larger shapes for comforting. An example: in 1945, when *Amazing Stories* published a "factual" article by Richard Shaver, an exposé of the civilization that lives inside our (hollow) Earth, the number of letters from readers leaped from forty a month to twenty-five hundred and stayed that way for the next four years while the Shaver reports continued. In the Earth live "Deros," evil creatures whose "tech machines" shoot rays that cause our wars and traffic accidents, our cancer and our sexual dysfunction. When "a hobo is arrested while attempting to wreck a train because a 'voice' directed the action"?—*Deros at work!* Like Satan's minions, they relieve us—they relieve a Vonnie Coleman—of a pure responsibility.

Or maybe Tasha will join up with the saucer-spotting priest, awaiting the Grand Arrival, the day salvation will simply be handed over to us, no questions asked, and those who want can leave this vale of suffering in the rounded titanium belly of the Mother Ship. In this cosmology, Jesus Christ is the greatest extra-terrestrial of all.

She'll see it—that Organizational Shapes, recurrent matrices, cannot be escaped. They form a unity on macrolevels as surely as we're the momentary cohering of subatomic particles, dot and wave, that dance their stately pavanes in the least of our gestures.

She'll see it—but not now. Now, she walks at night through

the house she was born in, whimpering at its familiarity, stopping a moment to feel her own self beat like an ocean in storm at her own self's borders, and clutching—actually pantomiming clutching—her pain to her breast.

I'm going to stretch next to Skyler tonight and love her with all of the luck we've been given (so far) and I suggest you set down this page and do that with somebody too.

Who *is* it we see when we look in the mirror, that rounds the weary corners of our own eyes, furtively, gone in an instant? *Wild man, mild man, monster, saint.*

This began with the Egyptian Old Kingdom, 2500 B.C., and it can end there well enough. I have a textbook of "religious art through the centuries," and it starts with the wingéd *ka*—a form of soul—as it flutters over a Pharaoh inside the tomb. It looks like a fledgling hawk, though with the head of a human: the face is concerned.

Many pages later, there's a sample of Marc Chagall's *Message Biblique.* Perhaps you know it: the world, the sky, are done from a palette of pinks, an urgent damask, a more rougey pastel, the range of rose and pouting shell-lip, pink, all pink. And through these heavens glides a single angel bearing a candelabrum. All of the suffering she's seen becomes the accent-lines of her eyes and mouth, with a tenderness. Her face is deeply green: against such pink, she's like green fire.

Is it a prayer? I don't know; it's annealing.

The Lake

"Poetry in Porkopolis"—so says the review in a Philly paper.

So far, four slim issues have appeared. *She* thinks they're harbingers, presentiments—of what, she isn't certain, but she knows they sputter raw, unheralded thought waves through the chill Chicago air, that they're transmitters, that they're *of* the times.

The angels of this later age are radio beams, exuberant twentieth-century angels, long as light is long; they'll sing in a box on the sitting room mantle, and they'll streak their way past the Twins and the Swan. The angels of this later age are dirigibles and biplanes. Angels like these require new high priests and priestesses, new seeing.

It's February 1913. Harriet Monroe is in the offices of *Poetry,* exalted *cum* depressed in a kind of emotional tossed slaw, as she investigates the morning's mail: laurels and brickbats, warbles of adulation and derisively rich Bronx cheers.

"So, Alice . . ." (this is Alice Corbin, her associate) "do we stride ahead through the end of the year, or refund our guarantors' charity?"

Alice says nothing; Alice continues to look from the Cass Street office window into one of those bleak Chicago winter skies the color of yesterday's alewife scales. The answer is obvious to Alice: this is Harriet Monroe, a quiet reed of a lady who's going to rub those dowdy Philadelphia noses into the living poetry meat of Porkopolis until its tang is appreciated.

Harriet Monroe: the Gertrude Steinian'd, Albert Einsteinian'd, wunderkind, cube-kissed, modernist spirit is on her; the rah-rah Dada hoodoo-lips of 1913 are readying to juicily play a rootie-toot-toot on the quiet reed in the head of this quiet reed of an editor-lady.

New winds are blowing.

In 1913, Igor Stravinsky's *The Rite of Spring* premiered at the Théâtre des Champs Élysées. "It marked the beginning of modern music." We know that now. "By mid-century it had become part of the standard symphony repertoire."

Yes. But that night, audience member Gertrude Stein, amidst the booing, witnessed one of the apoplectic gentlemen near her smash his cane into the top hat of an agitated neighbor. A woman elegantly cascaded in diamonds slapped the hissing man beside her. Cards were exchanged, for duels. A rain of catcalls fell to the stage, and choreographer Nijinsky stood on a chair in the wings, hands megaphoned at his lips, to scream the rhythm so his dancers could remain in synch with music that they couldn't—for the great affront and ruckus—even hear.

And does Stravinsky look so *very* revolutionary, seated with his hands in a casual clasp, in the drawing Picasso did?—a bookish-looking dandy of a man (Picasso, delightedly effervesced by the composer's mustard-yellow trousers and yellow shoes), his thinning hair and saucery glasses lenses. In his head, though, was the whomp-and-thump: it's not, after all, as if Harriet Monroe sat for her portraits breathing visible fire. (She had it, though.)

Everything then, it seems, was revolutionary. Of Igor Stravinsky: "He radiated that he was one of the men of the future." Stuck in the present, border guards at the Italian frontier at Chiasso checked his luggage in a routine search and confiscated that carefully rolled-up portrait Picasso had made a gift. They saw it as a military map.

And Picasso . . . ? In 1913 he and Braque are inventing new

eyes—bee-eyes, omnifaceted eyes—for the world. His *Bottle of Vieux Marc, Glass, and Newspaper* (actual newspaper, pasted and pinned) is 1913, ditto *Student with a Newspaper,* ditto *Glass and Bottle* by Braque, as well as Braque's *Woman with a Guitar* and *Guitar and Program.*

1913: Joyce is working on *Dubliners,* Eliot on "The Waste Land."

1913: Lawrence publishes *Sons and Lovers.* Frost, *A Boy's Will.* Willa Cather, *O Pioneers,* and Joseph Conrad, *Chance. The Tempers* (William Carlos Williams). Whomp-and-thump. Marcel Proust: *Swann's Way.*

Everything caught in the toppledown, reorganizing wind.

Stravinsky wriggling like an inchworm through a window at the rear of the Théâtre, on the lam from his own melee.

When we think about the past, we need a pattern. Need to survey those millennia of unprecedented invention, and call it the Neolithic. Take its tongue-curl fear and its blood-on-fire glories, and find in them a system: they mean such-and-so. My years in the clergy, we say. The months that were strung like beads on the thread *divorce,* we say. The Dark Ages. The Renaissance.

Because of my own homegrown predispositions, I see dots of 1913 constellated into meaningful shapes we tend to call "High Art."

On other days, the funky, junky hellzaboomin' cellar end of the scale may be as rife with ripe events. In 1913 ingenue Krazy Kat and nemesis/sweetiepie Ignatz Mouse are given (after longtime second-banana status as filler for *The Dingbats*) their own comic strip. "It continued to be published through World War I, the Roaring Twenties, the Great Depression, and World War II—a run of thirty-one years. Among comic strips it is a certifiable masterpiece. In the world of art and literature it is an innovation." (Picasso was wild about it.)

1913: Edgar Rice Burroughs is high on the fan mail pouring into the offices of the crock-o'-schlock *All-Story:* in that middle-level pulp 'zine, he's just published his brainchild, *Tarzan of the Apes,* and now he's awaiting his editor's first words on its sequel. *Under the Moons of Mars* is also in *All-Story;* but should he pursue this ability full-time? (It's a question that torments him as did that of filial retribution for Hamlet.)

Or it might be the sciences, either applied or theoretical. 1913: Danish physicist Niels Bohr successfully maps the atom's vasty nothingness and rings of orbit whizzery; of Bohr's model that year of the hydrogen atom, Einstein later wrote that it "appeared to me like a miracle."

1913: Sigmund Freud is the author of *Totem and Taboo.*

1913: William M. Burton receives a patent for a process in which oil is converted to gasoline. In Highland Park, Michigan, Henry Ford predicts that his new idea, a "moving assembly line," 250 feet in length, will fully quadruple his current production of Model T's.

The future is seeded. The century is zooming. We need to see it this way.

Or it simply might be the Omaha tornado of 1913, which created a canyon five miles long through the center of the city on that year's Easter Sunday. *To My Dear Sis,* says the slanted hand on the back of a locally printed photograph postcard, *oh sis you can never imagine what it was like. By By Dollie.*

Patterns: for the rest of his life, he'll see his days in terms of funnels, in terms of sun and then fulminous dark. There won't be a week that he doesn't wake from a dream of his wife's hand looking like a shrub growing out of the rubble.

On February 17, 1913, at the armory of the Sixty-ninth New York Regiment on Lexington at Twenty-fifth, an International Exhibition of Modern Art took place—the famous "Armory Show"

that liberated American tastes from what had been over a century of complacency.

Matisse, Duchamp, Cézanne, Van Gogh, John Marin, Kandinsky, Francis Picabia, Odilon Redon, Braque, Brancusi, Gaugin—they entered American consciousness here, for the first time, having something like the effect of a "Composition for Whoopee Cushion and Pinwheel Fireworks" suddenly bursting forth from a chamber quartet. (Also among the catalog's 1,270 listed items were those by a "Paul" Picasso.)

The slogan of the show: "The New Spirit." "I went to it and gasped along with the rest," said William Carlos Williams. Ninety thousand attended over the month of the Show and were given the whammy, the quick-kick-to-the-pineal-gland, by futurism, expressionism and cubism, out of nowhere it seemed, and at once. Martin Green calls their varied aesthetics a "repudiation of recognizableness."

When Mabel Dodge, who ably primed both energy and money for the Show, wrote Gertrude Stein three weeks before its doors were opened to the public, she called it the "most important event that has ever come off since the signing of the Declaration of Independence, and it is of the same nature." As she put it later: "I was going to dynamite New York and nothing would stop me." (Store this image: eventually we'll return to it.)

On closing night, when the last of the dazzled spectators had been led away from *Nude Descending a Staircase*—hooting or razzing or nearly devotionally silent, each according to his or her accommodation—the doors were locked from within, and the Sixty-ninth Regiment fife and drum corps played, as a larger regiment of at-attention magnums of champagne were wheeled into the center room.

Somebody costumed-up in a knee-length beard and a Lincoln stovepipe hat weaved through the crowd with an exaggerated palsy, claiming to be the representative of the National Academy of Design. They took turns whirling him in a turkey trot. Then everyone—janitors, ticket sellers, artists, impresarios, wan intelligentsia, guards, and guides alike—grabbed hips and "followed the painter Daniel Putnam Brinley in a snake dance through the rooms."

This is the same tune being hammered away on brainplates simultaneously from hither to half-past-yon. In Chicago, Harriet Monroe is one more 1913 note in a music clamoring—now whispering—now wockawocka hoochiecooing the planets out of their courses—under the capable, inescapable maestroleadership of Professor Zeitgeist, consummate conductor.

("*Sight kites,* dollink?" Krazy inquires of Ignatz, staring up at her newsprint sky.)

But there are lulls in this music; in that quietus, indecision wells.

The editorship of *Poetry* is no fulltime job—as yet. As art reviewer for the Chicago *Tribune,* Harriet Monroe is just returned from viewing the Armory Show and, half against her will, is sore dismayed.

Matisse is "fundamentally insincere" and an "unmitigated bore," and his work consists of "the most hideous monstrosities ever perpetrated in the name of long suffering art." Cézanne is "the shabby French vagabond," Van Gogh "the half-insane Flemish recluse and suicide," Gaugin of course "disreputable." The Show is good—for a laugh. She says on February 23, "If these groups of theorists have any other significance than to increase the gayety of nations your correspondent confessed herself unaware of it."

And yet . . . she stares at her desk. Those canvases, so patched with jagged shards of color . . . They stick in her mind. That's what shards do, she says, what shards are *supposed to do.* Art shrapnel.

Very uneasy, this reed of a lady. Color straight from the tube, great gouts of color pouring out of the faucet . . .

She stares at her desk as if its sea-green blotter might, with concentration, turn transparent, letting bits of wisdom bobble up to the top. She toys with a recent gift to the office, a Pegasus molded in rich lead crystal.

"Alice? I think I'll go for a brief perambulation down at the lake." She points to her pile of letters and poems, and gives her wrist a shrug that says the arbitration of such as *these* would be beyond even the veriest Solomonic of wisdoms. "You know how the lake air sweeps my thinkum clean again."

Alice says nothing, but kindly so. Harriet buttons her lamb's wool coat to the chin. "I'll return in the hour."

Alice knows that we're as tumbleweeds in the winds of the times, and that withersoever they blowest, we rollest. Harriet leaves, a gray coat in a brisk gray gust of February.

Think about the pioneering Norwegian polar explorer Fridtjof Nansen—how he made his three-year-long, three-thousand-mile circuit of formerly untraveled Arctic waters by intentionally freezing his ship into drift ice, letting it bear this fleck.

That's how I see the zeitgeist working—carrying us, the many flecks, though some don't know they're in motion, and some are farther behind, and some in advance.

The year the call came saying the cancer had spread from my mother's lungs to her shoulder and back, I saw the world in terms of cancer: that was my template. Everything radiated death. A friend gave birth to a healthily yawling girl, a thing of immense pink beaming: even that, somehow, I managed to see in the shadow of bereavement. When a creampuff-hairdo'd news anchor coughed—a quick dry nothing—that was just a symbol of my mother's cough, that tearing up of the wet cells of her lining.

When you're in the Mob, then the world is the Mob, and the rest of the world is not-Mob: that's the code. When you're a Hassid Jew, the least impossible cheese mite of Creation is proof of your universe, and your every stale or scented breath, your fuck-breath and your boredom-breath, these all are the breaths of a Hassid Jew.

Every day, we prescribe ourselves lenses.

When the President flickered onto the screen and said that call-in radio shows were spreading hate through the nation like a can-cer—I wept all day.

So cold, on the ice. So cold—and the wind in its single di-rection.

This is what I learned: that courage, and charity, comfort, and concern—are only the little c's.

In 1913, *Arts and Decoration* gave its March appearance over to the Armory Show. Included were both an essay by Gertrude Stein called "Portrait of Mabel Dodge at the Villa Curonia" and, as a complement, Mabel Dodge's essay on Gertrude Stein—who was, said Dodge, "prodigious. Pounds and pounds and pounds piled up on her skeleton—not the billowing kind but massive, heavy fat . . . her body seemed to be the large machine that her large nature required to carry it." Her laugh was "like a beefsteak."

She'd be laughing it more, and more openly, now. She was fi-nally her complete self. This was the year that her brother Leo moved out of their house on the rue de Fleurus, leaving Paris for Settignano. February: he sold his Picassos, gingerly packed six-teen Renoirs and two Cézannes, and then was gone—his own enormous width of physical presence, in its absence, seeming to open up extra rooms.

Not that he'd subjugated his steamroller sister; who *could?* Still, in the days when they were inseparable, it was Leo who al-ways expatiated, Leo who made the polysyllabic point to the mes-merized acolyte. Now, the future begins: it's Gertrude now, and Alice B. Toklas, sitting iconographically in the gaslight on salon nights, sometimes waking with each other in the bed beneath Pi-casso's *Hommage à Gertrude*. (Was he thinking of the apartment's few bronze Buddhas? Surely he's painted her as pounds and pounds and pounds of Buddha.) "I was alone at this time in understanding [Picasso]," she wrote later, "perhaps because I was expressing the same thing in literature."

"The Stein salon was, among other things, a kind of echo chamber in which certain enthusiasms and art theories and reputations were enhanced, intertwined, and further mystified at the expense of the intellectually insecure. It was also an anteroom where would-be disciples waited in hope of meeting the painters themselves, in hope of entering their world. The painters were the source of all truth and the focus of all glamour."

Now the beefsteak laugh is frequent, and seasoned with what she calls—she wanted it always, and now at last she has it—*la gloire*.

✦

For some, the arrival of glory is more recalcitrant. In February 1913 Edgar Rice Burroughs sits in his office at the Chicago branch of the magazine *System* (Wabash and Madison Avenues), surveying his future. *Dismal* is the word, at least if the present and past are an index.

System calls itself "the magazine of business." For an annual fee of fifty dollars, a businessman can write to *System's* Service Bureau as often as he likes, for detailed counsel on any dilemmas. Burroughs's job is to write this counsel—and yet "I knew little or nothing," he'd say in his *Autobiography*, "about business, had failed in every enterprise I had ever attempted and could not have given valuable advice to a peanut vendor."

This is history, not modesty. It officially begins in 1895 with his stint as bill collector for the Knickerbocker Ice Company (returning one day to where he's tied his horse, he discovers it's eaten the leaves completely off the trees of Lieutenant Bondfield of the Chicago Police Department). That fall, he's appointed Professor of Geology at the Michigan Military Academy ("needed a Professor of Geology and I was it . . . the fact that I had never studied geology seemed to make no difference whatsoever").

In 1897 his patient father is helping him receive his early discharge from the cavalry. A stationery store in Pocatello, Idaho, fails (the Good Lord "never intended me for a retail merchant!"). Cattle herding. Treasurer of his father's American Battery Company. Dredging gold at Stanley Creek in the Sawtooth Mountains. Railroad cop for the Oregon Short Line Railroad in Salt Lake City ("Can't say I am stuck on the job"). Crawling steel girders for a seventeen-story warehouse under construction. Peddler, door to door, of "Stoddard's Collected Lectures." Selling candy ("Flops"). Light bulbs ("Flops"). He's recently pawned his watch. He hawks Alcola, a patent-medicine "cure for alcoholism." Corsets ("Flops"). Pencil sharpeners ("Flops"). Some diary entries: *Head aches for years—No lunches—Great poverty—Am just about ready to give up.*

Now with two accepted stories but even more rejections sliding about confusedly in his noggin; and bambino number three on the way; and the news this morning, February 15, 1913, that George Tyler Burroughs, his father, who's seen him patiently through all of this two-bit uselessness, is dead at age seventy-nine . . .

. . . the creator of Tarzan lets the cold waft into his propped-up *System* window. He moans at his memo-strewn desk like an animal struck in the road as the 1913 bandwagon nattily speeds along . . .

. . . a croak of a note, another out-of-synch espousal of self-doubt in the otherwise snappily confident, to-the-moon-and-back tune of the times.

The future is always being created. (So is the past.) Why does it seem—somehow—this year—the future is being created *more?*

In 1913 the U.S. income tax law goes into effect.

The *New York World* introduces the "crossword puzzle."

Grand Central Station opens; so does the Panama Canal.

A man named Cecil B. DeMille, in search of a spot to shoot his first "movie," a Western, nixes his original location—Flagstaff, Arizona—and chooses instead a sleepy, unpretentious California town called Hollywood.

President Wilson delivers the first in-person State of the Union address in 112 years.

1913: it's a blueprint of "tomorrow"; it's a great dividing cell.

Yes, but when Edgar Rice Burroughs walks off the job at the seventeen-story warehouse under construction, somebody else is tapped to fill his place, and this man stinks of fear of heights for ten-hour days for the rest of his life—*he'll* tell you what it takes to bring a blueprint to completion.

And as for "dividing cell," not the metaphor, no, but the real uterine thing that you'd see on a lab smear, that you'd smell on a middle finger . . . aren't there wadded-up cotton balls in a Paris brothel that are actually—in a line of direct causation—the engine that powers some of Picasso's savviest canvases?

I'm trying to say that the gleaming, lightsome dreams of any era require somebody's heavily cranking up the dream-gears in the basement dankness.

1913: Gandhi is arrested. Russian revolutionary Josef Dzhugashvili signs his name for the first time as *Stalin* ("man of steel"). *Union organizer* and *anarchist* enter popular usage. Some refuse to forget that when Edgar Rice Burroughs quits his job as a railroad dick, another man is tapped to fill his place, who breaks his lantern over the head of a bum in the mouseshit dirt of a boxcar; every day this happens somewhere in the bottommost dark of 1913. Everywhere, rabble is ready for rousing.

The political spirit isn't unlike what one might find in the lab of Niels Bohr: a ferocious excitement, a newness—yes, but first, existing models need to be dismantled.

Here's an atom of social upheaval: on June 4, 1913—Derby Day—a suffragist named Emily Davidson brazenly sprinted onto the track at Epsom Downs directly in the path of the King's prize horse, attempting to seize its reins. She was trampled to death: a martyr to her cause.

The month before, ten thousand had marched in New York on behalf of women's voting rights. Guerrilla suffragists cut major telephone lines (the London–Glasgow cable went in February of 1913), mutilated designated national treasures, set the homes of politicos afire; one diehard threatened Winston Churchill with a whip. When jailed, they hunger struck—they were bound and forcibly fed with metal funnels like geese.

In Chicago, Charles Moyer, outspoken president of the Miners Union, was shot in the back and dragged through the streets. I have the reproduction of a photograph from 1913: freshly painted, a one-horse advertising wagon poses at a curb, the SOCIALIST CARAVAN, traveling COAST TO COAST in the hope of stirring up 2,000,000 VOTES IN 1916 FOR THE SOCIALIST PARTY. 1913: February 5, a seventeen-year-old garment worker, Ida Braeman, was shot (to death) in the chest while demonstrating peacably with a group of strikers in front of a Rochester tailor shop. Their demands were for an eight-hour day and overtime pay. She had planned to announce her wedding engagement that evening.

Ida Braeman—a Jew. The new winds carried *shtetl* smells and the goods-hawking squawk of a peddler oratorio. March 31 of 1913 proved itself a record immigration day at Ellis Island: 6,745 impatient embodiments of alien need and alien energy entered under the sign of Liberty's come-on torch; by May, the previous-nine-month total was 900,000.

Coarser voices enter the chorus, ghettospeak patois (*"Pat oys,"* says Krazy Kat, and heavy on the *oy.*) Professor Zeitgeist striking up a ragtag carny band of banjo and washboard, blues and klezmer—striking up a martial air, a blat of the brass with the force of fists inside it.

1913: Robert Hayden is born. Ralph Ellison a year later. Darker streams of the American current. Harlem nights and demeaning niggertown days.

In 1913 George McManus's comic strip *Maggie and Jiggs*—that daffy, broguey love song to the upward-rising Irish—appears. (Jiggs's appetite introduces mainstream American tastes to corned-beef-and-cabbage.)

1913: Delmore Schwartz is born, who will carry his Jewishness commando-style into the halls of academe; and Karl Shapiro, author of *Poems of a Jew* (and who, in fact, will become the editor of *Poetry* in 1950).

New winds—and they bear the Old World garlic scent of my father in the kitchen at midnight, one night seventy years in the future, piling together an Irving Goldbarth special, the imprimatur of which is a redolent *greps* (a belch) and a very soulfully appreciative sound he always called, on making it, a "shmecka-da-lips." (I can hear it now.)

I'm there too, in that future. I'm thirty-eight and my father is going to die.

When Judy determined she'd leave for a year in Japan, I (sadly) equally determined I'd support her in this, in whatever small symbolic ways I could. That was the summer of bricks of green tea stacked a foot high in the kitchen; a potted bonsai—just about the size of the heart's small bramble of arteries—at the front door; a kimono on the doorknob at the bathroom, all of its misty mountain peaks and whiskery orange fish while Judy showered her trim American jogger's body behind the fogging curtain and I sat in bed imagining the apartment empty of all of this, and of her.

Now that was Austin, Texas—gift shops filled with armadillos welded out of pop tops. Finding even *kitschy* Japaneseiana wasn't easy. But I did it. I was thirty-eight and fresh from the muck of divorce, and Judy's sly and saucy twenty-two was fuse enough in the craziness for sudden love to blast me out of reality. I'd have chopped my left leg off and fashioned a hillock of sushi from it, if she'd wanted.

But she *didn't* really want anything, not from me, except a non-committal, background kind of "being there." Her yearnings by then were all Far East, and the summer was merely a block of months to wait through. I already missed her: I *pre*-missed her. With her ringleted head on my chest and the oozes of sex still slick around our thighs, I already mourned her absence. I would stroke her so hard I could feel the shape of the bones—the precious ivory smuggled into my life that I'd have to pay back. So this became the screen through which I saw each minute: Japan and bereavement. Zen and stir-fry and haiku and loss.

It's what we always, *always* do, it's what our brains are wired to do from even before our natal push down the chute: take welter, and force enabling order into its details. How from all of the numbers, *every* number, every *combination* . . . we will blow for luck on our hands, and bet a specific six or eleven, or whatever, is going to absolutely declare itself on the rolled bones. Into tumult, we structure these rungs through a day. (In excess, this becomes the skewed obsessing of conspiracy theorists: *Kennedy* has seven letters, so does *Lincoln*, etc.)

On the morning I drove Judy to the bus, I knew her "year" in Japan exempted her from my ongoing life forever. "Moshi-mosh" I said, and kissed her a last time, in my drear confusion using the phrase she'd taught me for their telephone "Hello." And then began the months of aimlessness and hungers.

When the phone call came from Chicago saying my father had died—the leukemia won that race ahead of his unreliable heart—of course I flew in the following morning. I cried, I held my mother as *she* cried, and my sister, and I flung the ritual handful of dirt down the graveshaft. But the truth is (though I'd loved him) that my grief was partially *labored* into existence, yes, and never fit my insides square and true: I'd been experiencing the world in a certain preestablished pattern, and his dying didn't fit.

I watched my mother as I clumsily recited the Jewish "mourner's prayer": she wasn't really here, *she* was transported by his death to somewhere untouched by anything cognitive. One night before I left their house, as I wandered it in the darkness while my mother and sister fitfully slept, I thought I saw—this lasted a second only—a ghost-him stand in the kitchen, layering up a deftly done ghost-sandwich. *It's okay,* he winked. He'd always forgiven me everything.

When the news arrived for Picasso, "he was in such emotional turmoil that he could not work." Eva wrote to Gertrude Stein, "I hope that Pablo will make himself start working again, because only this will help him forget his pain a little." And he did, and the world in its omnidirectional energies went onward from that moment when it had stopped—it always stops at the death of a parent, in this case Don Ruiz Blasco. It was May 3, 1913.

But the universe doesn't have a "theme," a "plot." Interpretation is a sliver in its slipstream.

1913: as the nations whet their blood-blades for the first of their World Wars, the news in Arvada, Colorado, on December 12 is snowbanks eight feet tall. Or another photo postcard sent that year: "127 Rattlesnakes Killed in One Day. Near Dupree South Dakota." (They're draped on a handheld pole so laden, it needs a second pole to be angled under it as a cross-support.)

1913: Chaplin makes his film debut (as a villain). The Kaiser bans the tango. Mount McKinley is scaled ("the highest point on the North American continent"). A statistician working for Prudential Life "declares cancer a national menace." In New Mexico a grasshopper cloud is reported, five miles by eighteen miles: for anyone caught in its biblical thunder, the revving gun-planes of Germany must have been planets and planets away.

Small things. In 1913 the Noesting Pin Ticket Company, then of Mount Vernon, New York, was founded. Henry Lankenau's patent for "the Gothic clip" was assigned to that farsighted business concern; today, it claims to have made "the world's largest selection of paper clips for over 75 years." Its catalog includes the Gem, the Frictioned Gem, the Perfect Gem (you'd *think* one needn't proceed from that), the Marcel Gem, the Universal Clip (again, you think . . . but, ah!), the Nifty Clip, the Peerless Clip, the Ring Clip, and the Glide-on Clip.

Elsewhere, the perfected design called "Hookless No. 2" was unveiled. Quoting Henry Petroski: "U.S. Patent No. 1,060,378, issued in 1913, is now often taken as the milestone marking the introduction of the zipper." Looking—as well it should, in its ancestralness—like a trilobite risen from stone.

Small things. In 1913 D. H. Lawrence is wintering at Gargnano, Lago di Garda: "There is a great host of lemons overhead, half visible, a swarm of ruddy oranges by the path, and here and there a fat citron. It is almost like being under the sea."

The Armory Show was over in the middle of March. June 7, under the leadership of the International Workers of the World, the striking silk mill shleps of New York and New Jersey—many of them Polish and German Jews with ties to socialist traditions, and Italians who honored a history of fiery activism—produced what's come to be called the Paterson Strike Pageant. Twenty-five hundred marched up Christopher Street and Fifth Avenue, singing the "Marseillaise" and the "Internationale," as led by an eighteen-year-old worker, Hannah Silverman.

What were they asking for really? Decent lives. And what was the answer? Local and state militias, and the clubs of the police.

An old, old story: its statistics are repeatedly on record through the centuries.

But this, as a response, was new. You could feel the waves of calories break out of that unstoppable parade. It led to Madison Square Garden, rented for that one night. "In 1913 it was a magnificent Renaissance building, in cream-colored brick and terra-cotta trim and with arcades copied from Italy on both the street level and the roof garden. On top of the tower stood a sculpture of Diana by Saint-Gaudens . . ." (Martin Green). The Pageant organizers had spelled IWW in red lights placed around all four sides of the tower, keeping this secret until the last moment, until it was too late for authorities to find and unthrow the switch. It burned, a declarative torch, for all of Manhattan to see.

Twelve hundred workers had parts on stage, for an eager audience of over fifteen thousand (nearly a thousand needed to stand). "The air was electric." There were six scenes, all enacted in front of the same two-hundred-foot backdrop of a dismal Paterson silk mill, prison-gray and prison-weighty; the stumbling narrative goes from zombie workers lumbering in for another day's demands, through various stages of increasing self-awareness and rebellion. By the end of the Pageant, the audience joined the performers in singing strike songs and in cheering Wobbly heroes, and in hissing and booing the mellerdrama police. The whole building: a raw red throat of festive indignation.

And who were the forces behind this historic event? Bill Haywood, Elizabeth Gurley Flynn, John Reed and Carlo Tresca—all of them, mixers-uppers at the Mabel Dodge salon. As the merits of cubism flew through that room and were denounced or exalted, there was the dapper Tresca, for instance, someone who'd been "arrested 37 times for blasphemy, sedition, criminal obscenity, conspiracy, and murder; and was shot at, bombed, kidnapped by fascists and had his throat cut" (hence the waggish beard?).

In the Mabel Dodge apartment at 23 Fifth Avenue, corner of

Ninth, the Armory Show and the Pageant were equally welcome, equally promulgated soundings of the times—they were a double-headed trumpet announcing one full-steam-ahead thing.

Around the bearskin rug in front of the white marble fireplace, below the Venetian chandelier—here, dissidents Emma Goldman and Margaret Sanger held forth (Dodge helped finance Sanger's incipient journal *Woman Rebel*); and painters John Marin and Picabia, and photographer Stieglitz, might be found enjoying the passed-around bottles of kümmel shaped like Russian bears. In 1913 Dodge presented Pageant dynamo (and enamorato) John Reed to Picasso and Gertrude Stein.

"Far apart as the Show and the Pageant stood, they spoke the same metamessage to the same people. For at that moment in history, art and politics came together, and so people's hopes and fears came together also. . . ."

Wedded in that wind! Professor Zeitgeist, with a fistful of batons. Strike up a marriage song!

". . . Since then, people have looked back to that moment in envy."

They were wedded that way in the minds of both supporters and detractors. They were whomp and thump and boomalayboom, of a piece. Green speaks of "a climate of strong hopes for . . . change for the better in all things. If by now [the Show and the Paterson Pageant] seem disparate and disconnected events, that is because we have lost touch with those hopes."

Yoking the two in condemnation, the *New York Times* said of the Armory Show, "It should be borne in mind that this movement is surely a part of the general movement to disrupt, degrade, if not destroy, not only art but literature and society too. . . . the Cubists and the Futurists are cousins to anarchists in politics." (One can hear the spat-out *ptooey.*) *Art and Progress* typified modernism: "the chatter of anarchistic monkeys." Enthusers used the same lingo, only giving it their own dervish, doctrinaire spin; and Hutchins Hapgood said of the Armory Show that he viewed it "as I would a great fire, an earthquake, or a political revolution; as a series of shattering events—shattering for the purpose of re-creation."

Hapgood again (on January 27, 1913): "There seems a vague but real relationship between all the real workers of our day. Whether in literature, plastic art, or the labor movement . . . we find an instinct to blow up the old forms and traditions, to dynamite the baked and hardened earth so that fresh flowers can grow." The image then was common (you'll remember I asked you to "store" away Dodge's saying, of her helping birth the Armory Show, "I was going to dynamite New York"). Or that famous supercilious newspaperese, of *Nude Descending a Staircase:* (*ptooey*) "an explosion in a shingle factory."

Duck, boys—here comes some art!

In Coconino County, on a blustery cartoon afternoon, those sharp art splinters streak through the sky, then slow, and float there coaxingly in the winds of the times, beseechingly, as if they would lead us upward, out of our blindness.

"*Sight kites,*" Krazy says. Seeing-eye creatures filling the air. If only we'd grab their tails.

With its farther shore invisible, and its water and air connected in intricate moodiness, Lake Michigan is nearly oceanic.

Today it was gray, the kind of February lake gray that will bluster out on the water and be unrelievable dullness at the shore rocks, somehow managing to even out of these two far states a monochromatic unity.

Harriet sat on a rock, and stared at the distant bluster. She was alone out here—you'd need to be wacky to sit at the lake today—

and what she really was doing, she knew, was staring into herself. For what?

"Some kind of reconciling," she said out loud, to no one.

"Pardon, ma'am?"

She was almost airborne at that.

"I didn't mean to frighten you, ma'am. Must be you didn't see me." Well *of course* she didn't, mister; he was hunkered-up on the rocks in a flat-gray overcoat (somewhat frayed, but also serviceable in a middle-class way: she noticed things like that), he could have been out here to *impersonate* a rock.

She must have studied him suspiciously, disdainfully suspiciously. "Well no offense intended, ma'am," (he'd sized her up: her own tycoonish dove-gray coat, and her bearing) "but you don't own the lake."

And she very well might have angered at that, or simply walked away—but, to her credit, she laughed, and then both of them laughed, and then they sat in their separate silences, waiting to see if there would be more. He had a heavy, *lumpen* jaw, she saw, but childlike sweet features floated above it. And although she desired her solitude, she also owed him a pleasantry; and so: "Tell me. Do you visit here often?"

"No ma'am, I don't. But I have," now doing something of a gesture that lassoed the overhead cloudiness, "thinking to do." Then, truly as if a child were suddenly to admit in a histrionic whisper *I have the Scabies* or *I have a frog named Hepzibah*: "I have Creditors." (And a father dead, he could have added.) "Creditors, and their collector bullies," he said, as if to himself— an almost singsong children's counting rhyme.

"Yes, money men can be *very* pusilanimous." Now with this summation, she thought their talk completed.

"*That's* a good word!" and a paper and pencil appeared in his hand from out of the coat—from out of a rock—as if he were a magician. He butt-sidled nearer to her, showed her he'd inscribed her accidental gift. By way of explanation he said, "I'm a *Writer*."

"Not a poet or a journalist, I trust. My head is populated enough by them."

"No ma'am. "I'm"—what? what *was* he, if he was *anything* deserving of the category at all? "I'm a teller of tales."

"Tall ones?"

"Very tall ones. One goes clear up to Mars."

"And are they persuasive, these escalatory tales?"

"You *do* use the words! Well, yes ma'am, two are published, with checks in the bank. But the question is . . ."

. . . and then he was confiding in her, copiously, a piping confessional gush not even Emma ever heard—after all, Harriet *was* an editor, and radiated discernment—starting, where?, oh gosh back in Idaho punching cows "I peacock-strutted about in Mexican spurs with inlaid ivory and silver dollar-sized rowels"—and horseshit duty ("No offense, ma'am: I meant it literally") in the cavalry—and serially onward—every failed bottom-grubbing work load whether clerkly or spit-&-sweat—the whole balloon armada of high hopes bursting one by one—but not just failure, no, he admitted, it also bespoke a wanderlust, a need to take the nowness of his life into the next thing—into newness—she was listening keenly now—she was a reed of a lady angled *into* the force of this prolixity—and it was this newness, it was the flow, that nourished him—but now with baby numero three (and a father dead, he could have added)—now with this writing thing—he talked of *ape*-men and *green* men—crackpot-silly, he knew—he loved it—half ashamed—it paid the bills—for a moment it did, but—

"May I ask your name?"

"I'm sorry, ma'am. It's Edgar. Ed."

"How old are you, Ed?"

A pause: because he knew he'd been sounding like some poor mooncalf. "Thirty-eight."

"It's time you settled down, I believe. It's time you stuck to one thing."

"Yes, yes, of course. But *is it the writing thing?*"

She looked inside him then, with that invasive critical eye of hers, she looked the way she'd hoped to look inside herself, at her own interior bluster. He held still, as if for an oil portrait. A minute went by—that's a very long time, on a naked rock in late February lake wind.

"Yes. Do the writing, Ed. Do the writing."

This was said in such finality, it came with an oracular ring, and it clearly sealed the end of their conversation. He was glad, for he took kindly to this woman, but felt embarrassed now at his self-exposure. And she—? desired her solitude.

To be polite he asked, "Can *I* help *you* in your cogitating, ma'am?"

She made a little wry lasso-twirl with her hand, and mimicked bringing in some of the far-out lake air closer.

"Thank you, Ed, but we have done all we can for each other."

And so they nodded understandingly, and he retreated a small ways up the shore. She continued to stare out into the distance . . .

Chicago poet Paul Carroll:

> . . . the lake,
> Green and gray as the color of some ghosts,
> Kept cracking against the rocks on the beach at Fullerton
> Like a practice of swords among the Caliph's Guard.

—*that's* my Lake Michigan! If you stare like a gypsy wisdom-woman into its crystal heart, its there and not-there heart, its always-been and never-was centrality . . . you can see the forge, the wellspring cuntlife genesis where Earth and Aether cohabit, and where the living and the dead are veins of the same ineffable state, and mingle, there in the Great Salon that never sleeps and is beyond what we call time.

A flicker: she saw he was ready to leave.

"Ed!"

"Yes?"

"There's only one s at the start of *pusillanimous*."

"Thank you, ma'am. I'll get better."

✦

1913: Ezra Pound introduces Yeats to Japanese No drama.

1913: Ezra Pound is married.

1913: Yeats composes and publishes "September 1913" in the *Irish Times*.

1913: Norway gives women the vote (the United States required seven years more: three more than Soviet Russia).

1913: Arthur Eddington, at Cambridge, assumes the Plumian Chair of Astronomy (he will soon describe the sun's internal structure, the actual *how* and *why* of its lightworks, for the first time).

1913: *Bicycle Wheel* by Marcel Duchamp ("the first piece of modern art employing motion").

1913: "As a last resort, a Michigan surgeon implants a dog's brain in a man's skull."

1913: Richard Nixon is born; jazzman Lionel Hampton; brewer Adolphus Busch; Albert Camus.

1913: Author Edgar Rice Burroughs zippily finishes writing eight novels: *The Return of Tarzan, At the Earth's Core, The Monster Men, The Cave Girl, The Warlord of Mars, The Mucker, The Mad King,* and *The Eternal Lover.* (The Ballantine editions of Burroughs in the 1990s are claiming "It is conservative to say . . . that of the translations into 32 known languages, including Braille, the number [of his books] must run into the hundreds of millions.")

1913: The nexus of the Armory Show is exhibited at the Art Institute of Chicago in March and April, where the ridicule exceeds New York's (the Institute's director quietly slips out of town beforehand). There are a few lonely advocates. One of them writes in the *Sunday Tribune* of April 6: "A number of protests against the present international exhibit have been printed in the newspapers. . . . The present critic, being one of those who, after seeing the exhibition in New York, strongly advised its being shown in Chicago, believes these protests to be ill-advised."

It's Harriet Monroe, Champion of Revitalizing Winds. And she'll write in *Poetry:* "The old prosody is a medieval left-over, as completely out of relation with the modern scientific spirit as astrology would be if solemnly enunciated from the summit of Mount Wilson. All the old terms should be scrapped."

In the Cass Street office, she lifts that Pegasus paperweight: *so* heavy! Such an impossible chunk of gravity! And yet somehow, it's flying.

If time is linear, art is linear: narrative, perspective and horizons. Knowledge is linear: lines of books. / If time is cyclical, art is circular. / If witches are possible, witches are actual: best set white-hot embers at their soles! / A culture's understanding of "gravity" is manifest in its scientific texts and in its architects' imaginations, equally—in its angels and its warships. / When a model exists, experience fits that model. / Who we love, we love because of what we love already (or what we don't). / The battle every day is versus Randomness, and this we face with the same assurance by which we fashion gods and sexpots, saints and serpents, out of the infinite chaos of the stars.

In Carl Barks's justly famous saga *Lost in the Andes,* Donald Duck (the Museum of Natural Science's "fourth assistant janitor") uncovers a long-forgotten stash of square eggs ("Think of how easily they could be packaged and stored," a magnate says at Interglobal Eggs, "they would stack like bricks!"). Soon Donald, accompanied by triad nephews Huey, Dewey, and Louie, is off to Peru in search of the "region of the mist," and there they find the home of the eggs, Plain Awful, a lost-to-civilization hidden empire of (yes) cubic-bodied men and women, and cubic-bodied hens. The buildings are cubes. The loincloths: tablet-looking squares. The eggs, if they go bad, will cause a discomforting "ailment in which the gastric ducts tie themselves into square knots." Food is a cube on a square plate. Hats are little boxes. *Mais oui,* circles are taboo, and the gum-chewing nephews in their innocence blow three very sacrilegious bubbles, leading to many a plot conundrum, until the happy finale (everybody friends again, the ducks instruct the pleased Plain Awfulians in square dance).

Show me a year, and I'll show you a human need to systematize its contents. Show me eternity, and I'll show you a human need for "years."

1995: I drive the fourteen hours to Chicago. I'm me: before I stop at my mother's house (and really, it's on the way) I pass the offices of *Poetry,* on Walton Street now, and I nod in acknowledgment: it's been ceaselessly singing for eighty-three years, for over three generations' shaped breath.

And then I take the Outer Drive to Foster and, for three or four minutes, I idle at the lake. The air is clear today, as if weegee'd clean, and even so, the distant *x* I stare at has a viscousness about it. What tomorrow-sky is in the sky, is chipping away for release with its one-atom egg-tooth? Clear, the air. But weighted, and active, and involuted: a lung.

You see? "Breath," "lung." My mother is coughing herself away in respiratory units. And I'll sleep in the basement under that sound, and I'll visit her chemotherapist on Wednesday, and I'll wake from my sleep with my heart like a fist at my sternum, and I'll smile reassuringly for her as the burn of pain takes over another inch she abdicates, and I'll utter the usual pieties, and I'll see the year this way, this only way, and I'll force everything into that seeing.

One night, I step outside for a quick fresh breeze. I start to hum: a wail of a hum, a tiny, sad and tuneless tune-to-sift-the-dirt-by.

I'm a mouth harp, that's what I am. Professor Z. is bent to me, is playing an intimate music.

Snapping pennants! Vendors waving sugar-wafers and wursts!

At Griffith Field in Los Angeles, Georgia "Tiny" Thompson Broadwicke makes her final inspection of every last buckle and strap.

The year is 1913. She's about to become the first woman ever to parachute from an airplane.

The excitement tongues her skin.

Her name is going to live forever.

The Lemmix

It's 1995, and a recent paperback's silver raised cover text promises "wildly exotic love in a harsh and beautiful land." This is the ambience, too, of the famous 1921 Rudolph Valentino movie *The Sheik:* the rhythmic dunes, a counterpointing caravan line, all deepened in a gorgeously bloody sunset, all imbued with the romance of the pre-technological. But Agnes Ayres, who stars opposite Valentino, is shown in the clasp of the desert warrior wearing a very 1921 wristwatch—one of the earliest bloopers, though of course the term was unknown then. In the 1926 sequel, the error repeats: this time it's Valentino himself, burnoused and passionate, who sports the contaminant timepiece.

This is why my Grandma Nettie had to die, I believe. She'd arrived in the land of Liberty from a world of village donkey carts —in basic ways, was permanently fixed by that world's ethos and tempos—and, having lived through Kitty Hawk, and both World Wars, and into the age of Sputnik (I can picture her, dimly, as one small patch on the backdrop of my life, as my transistor radio's static curtain admits the top hit "Telstar" into the room), she became an embarrassment to Time, an outmoded unit.

She couldn't speak English. Her thick shoes laced up with a buttonhook. She knew what it was to sit in the kitchen and pluck a chicken bald to its stippled skin. She might as well have attended the world premier of this year's microchip Rolexes wearing a heavy miniature hourglass strapped to her wrist. And so, when the last of the cotton underthings had been stained for the last time, we buried her.

There aren't any photographs of her childhood; there were no cameras there and then, period. Really there's only one image of her that I know (her face less photographed by far than faces of certain pampas herdsmen or New Guinea weaver women, or that Neolithic-level tribe that *National Geographic* was snapping so gleefully about a decade ago).

The occasion, my parents' wedding. Already this woman who's nine months short of being a grandmother looks like an emptied pouch, although I'm tempted to also read a weary kind of dignity into her bearing. My father is beaming goofily through the 1947 tones of black and white. My mother is contentedly placid; her hat aspires to emulate an orchid plantation. Everyone must have been festive—I imagine my father czardashed to a neighbor's accordion far past sober accomplishment—but the clothing is that of the rising poor; and the table's offerings, similarly thin; and the room is some plainly-fixtured neighborhood hall within walking distance. No one in this photograph drove. In 1947, with the world accommodated by then to visions of atom-powered Flash Gordon rocket travel, the car was still a luxury to these people. It waited somewhere out there with moonships.

So I'm puzzled at this fuzzy demi-memory I have of Grandma Nettie appearing, surprisingly enough, in a jittery fifteen seconds or so of actual movie film. Unlikely, given her retrograde vibes. And yet it's certainly *possible;* Uncle Morrie was an engineer (by virtue of having any degree past grammar school, he declares himself in this narrative as someone unrelated by blood, who married into the family) and he toyed around with a clunky prototype camera-and-synchronized-tape-recorder-attachment intended for home use. In the last of her days, he might indeed have captured her, with rounded chopper in hand, above the great wooden bowl in her lap, in which the chicken liver and hard-boiled eggs and sprinkled nuggets of chicken grease and fist-sized onions were being made one. She looks up, and she says one blurry, Yiddish-phlegmy sentence that sounds to me like *Ahlaf seyna dokwanda*—"I have seen a dark wonder" is how I remember it.

She'd be dead soon after. Morrie is dead. His cutting-edge-of-a-movie-camera is long since superseded. Nothing stops the future from eating us alive and recombining us. Those zippy Flash Gordon astrocruisers are still the stuff of fantasy, but fifteen seconds of Nettie Goldbarth is beaming, along with *Gunsmoke* and *Your Hit Parade* and *The Honeymooners,* past the outermost ring of the planets and onward—a face (and a bowl of chopped liver) composed completely of photons now.

When Flash and Dale and Zarkov land on Mongo, what they find is a despotic ruler and subjugated peoples, what they find is violence, sexual passion, avarice, selfless sacrifice—the range of human doing that would be at home in Dickens, and that plays its capabilities out in a recognizable narrative progression. If the eyrie-spired city of the Hawkmen floats above Mongo on a pillar of "strato-thrust" . . . its halls are peopled (even if wingédly peopled) with character types whose motivations, foul or noble, are bred in the very chemicoghostly neural works that power the corner cop and the supermarket cashier.

Although the genre's best practitioners *can* be psychologically savvy, the commonest sci-fi (surely the pumped-with-wonder adventuresome stuff I read as a kid) predicts on the level of Nifty Scientific Doohickeys only, and assumes what I call the Electric Can Opener Noneffect: the move ("up"?) from a manual to an electric model, even to a model with lights and ergonomic Velcro grips and buzzers, is a matter of pure convenience; the actual *thinking* of the user doesn't alter. For most of us, and most sci-fi, a rocketship is a can opener.

The cover art of my twenty-five-cent 1953 Signet edition of

Asimov's *The Currents of Space* (which looks to my lay eye to be by Saunders or Valigursky, although it's uncredited) shows us plucky hero and heroine on the run through a future spaceport thrillingly filled with the visual cues that say Tomorrow. Other planets have been conquered: an impressive needle-with-thrusters spaceship sleeks straight up from a billow of rocket exhaust. A sister ship stands by, for clearance. A third ship scores an off-white feather of propulsive trail diagonally across the sky. Two small security rocket patrollers are zipping after our fleeing two-some at nearly ground level. The hero wears a grapely purple flight suit with its traditional fishbowl helmet, and the heroine's blouse's shoulders are given an aerodynamically futuristic three-tier look.

But our hero is also holding an oblong of carry-on leather luggage no different from what gets heaved to the docks in the golden age of steamship travel; in fact, it's colorfully covered with stickers that likely say Mars Dome 1 or Saturn City, but could be claiming Istanbul or Cairo just as well. Around his neck is the same damn traveler's camera my father would have brought along in 1953, when I was five and we vacationed at the Indiana Dunes.

We almost always think that future eyes—whatever electroluxury or nuevo-Boschian hovel they review us from—will marvel at our objects *(they had "cans"!)* and maybe customs *(and "vacations"!)* but connect to brains that necessarily function in a sequence and with oversensibility we'd recognize as kindred.

That assumption may be tested in the next few generations. No, can openers will not rewire the paths of the species' circuitry. The electric can opener *is* an easier opener, and our life goes on. But the car *isn't* simply an easier horse; and, after its invention, *different* life goes on, and different eyes are required to be its witness. The shape of the planet and how we understand it—change. Ideas having to do with needs so basic as sex and privacy—change. The speed of the car and the speed of a roll of movie film demand new speeds from change itself. Then okay, maybe even a can opener becomes part of a cultural complex. And we come to fit the shape of the exoskeleton that—by cathode ray and silicon chip and laser and fiber optic—we've made.*

"Embedded in every tool is an ideological bias," Neil Postman writes, "a predisposition to construct the world as one thing rather than another."

And our next change?—evolutionary. Not in a metaphorical sense, but a literal Darwinian one. The beings of the cyberhive, linked up in their achronal, nonsequential, and unspatial cyber-atmosphere, will surely repattern their brains' own storage and sparkage in terms of such context.

I don't think that this is "bad" any more than it's "good"—any more than the cosmos operates in terms of "up" and "down." But I do know where my fondness wells. I know that a certain orderliness, and a certain sense of individual definition, are passing away.

On page one of Asimov's *The Currents of Space,* somebody visits an office of the Interstellar Spatio-analytic Bureau. (Whew!) He's in another galaxy. (Double-whew!) And yet the stellar agent he talks to is waiting for response to some "letters"—writings, on papers, the kind my Grandma Nettie for all of her lack of formal education piled into a life's enabling building blocks, and which (no matter their hearty existence in Asimov's book) are quickly being marginalized and left like shoreside litter by our onrushing currents of consciousness.

We drove out to the Indiana Dunes in a 1951 Chevrolet that had the high-crowned rounded smoothness of a Stetson hat—an altogether admirable design, as I look back on it now, though it

---

*Is a can of pop twelve ounces because our human thirst is standardly twelve ounces? Or has our thirst learned to be satisfied as sized to a can of pop?

must have been a model from the bottom of the line at the time. My father was a studious driver, of many fussy attentions to the road and his machine; and this, I guess, was part reaction to his first chaotic stint behind the wheel. The story goes that Uncle Morrie taught him to drive by taking them out in Morrie's car some dozen miles, stopping, switching places, and saying, "Okay, Irv, now you take us back." It must have been one hell of a bucking ride.

I would have been, oh, seventeen or so when Morrie suddenly died of a heart attack, a healthy man who went down like a great tree. While I don't remember the funeral or the week of *shiva,* I clearly recall *his* mother, an elderly stocky-bodied Yiddish-speaking woman, dramatically planting herself in a doorway and moaning—staying there, unbudgeably in that niche as if it became an official moaning station, and venting a grief that was larger than she was. Once, in her Old World, damaged English: "No! That the mother lives more than the son—*no!*"

She was right: it broke the normal narrative flow, and she became anachronistic, she became (unbearably so) another wrong time strapped to a wrist.

These days, when I think of the death of the printed page (or at least, the death of its primacy), I invoke her large-scale moan, since I ascribe it to the pell-mell rush-to-death of a fantasy creature I've invented. Listen . . .

. . . Proponents of change will always see (and will proselytize, in its imagistic terms) a shining horizon. That shine, or blaze, or steady clarifying gleam, is seen as the light of the phoenix, lifting from its ashes in transmogrified exultance. Print culture dies; *a flash;* the on-line paradise rises.

That's as valid a trope as any—as valid as mine. But I prefer mine, I prefer it more each day as my few lifetime choices polarize: either the omniwhambangbuzzbuzzinforama—or the quiet and maestroly guidance of a single book in a cone of watts; the storyless imagebarrage of MTVese—or the serial, history-steeped accumulation of narrative language; the inter-rabble babblechat of the nownow everywhere colonymind—or one lone person's concentration on one invited exemplar of authorial ministration.

Out of the felt effects of a Gutenberg world that patterned the ethos of even trivial everyday *non*textual moments, my parents who never graduated from high school nonetheless structured a life for themselves and their children as solidly and yet modestly joindered together as paragraphs stitched to each other with sensible, supple transition statements. This is the world I care to honor; and this is the world that's disappearing, as *we're* disappearing, busy as we are, becoming other "we"s.

Jerry Mander: "Technologies have organized themselves in relation to other technologies to create an interactive web, of which we're only one part. We feed it, and we serve it, and we interact with it, and we co-evolve with it, and we slowly become it. We're practicing a form of intra-species suicide."

Before the phoenix splendiferously rises, the phoenix's death is required. The resurrection may be, indeed, a glory hallelujah thing, I admit—but to the part that dies, the death itself is everything. And the fantasy creature I've thought up is the lemmix—because the lemming is the necessary first half of the tale of altering states. And to the lemming, the tale is never pretty.

The brightness *I* see is the glint of the sun on the water as the pell-mell rush tumbles over the rim of the cliff. Ten billion Chevrolets is one more way I see it, driving determinedly off the edge of the world, and changing into invisible, bodiless blips of data in mid-air. And then I hear, above this scene, the moan—the moan of Morrie's mother, become the ionosphere, an overarcing elegy-moan. *Its* proper business isn't the life to come, but the life that's leaving.

✦

Not that I'm a proponent of some kind of cultural stay-in-place jellyfish float. Not that I'm a child of stasis.

If anything, the atomic go-go sparkle of the baby boom attended my birth in 1948, a year that also saw the patenting of the holograph and the transistor. In the glossary to the *Funk and Wagnalls 1948 Yearbook,* these new terms—as if still smoking with the press of creation—need to be defined: *aureomycin, chemosurgery, cosmotron, discophile, heliport, LP record, micronutrient, photocomposition, pollster, transistor, vitamin B-12.* Also on the list is *update,* "to bring up to date," already in its natal year a seemingly hopeless concept in an ever-vooming world. The continuous morphing of *that* into *this,* and of the humdrum into the ohwow, is my birthright.

I can see myself at thirteen, at the Hanukkah and Thanksgiving family get-togethers, absenting myself from the drone of dweeby adult conversation (psychologically, attitudinally, but not physically: I wouldn't have been allowed to leave the room) by plugging one ear into my pocket-size AM transistor radio: yes, and I'd hum at the end of that pale plastic umbilicus, sweetly imbibing the hot Top 40 playlist, tunes that must have seemed to me then to be the anthems by which a fierce and fearless generation would enter the gates of Tomorrow. It may as well have been a "cosmotron," not a radio from the dime store, and its rock-and-roll may as well have been the music by which the spheres of the heavens revolve.

Then why *didn't* I turn out to be like Rhinoceros? A 1969 issue of *Harper's* profiled that (then-) next-to-hit-it-Big rock band. The author, Sara Davidson, visits its sleepy-eyed jam sessions at their dilapidated upstate New York mansion, natters comfortably with their groupies, travels along to various gigs, like one at "the Aerodrome, a warehouse converted into a seedy psychedelic nightclub." She says, "While all the members of Rhinoceros have agile minds, none of them reads anything at all. Four had extensive training in classical music. Michael taught piano at age twelve, and Alan was composing chamber music at Chicago Musical College when he quit to join the band. But they don't read. It's as if the print medium, with its even lines, is too confining and too laborious. Danny says, 'My mind is always going so fast I can't get into books or stories or anything.'"

That's twenty-six years gone. They *didn't* make it Big. What they did, I'd bet, these boy-men who don't read and their equally bookophobic groupie loves, is raise a generation of children who, by now, are old enough themselves to vote, and sue, and screw, and raise their own Nintendo-trōpic broods with minds that are going so, so fast—too fast, in any case, for the turning of anything so outmoded as pages. These aren't fringe people I'm talking about—*these are* a valid version of the mainstream American dream as it's carried one quarter of a century in its swift sweep.

So it isn't surprising (although it's coincidental: this isn't a packaged-up "theme issue") that the same 1969 *Harper's,* in its cover story on *Time* magazine's misfortunes, says in its final, list-centered paragraph that "along with all the mundane, immediate problems, there's always McLuhan and his electric circuitry. Are print culture's hot linear days numbered? Will post-industrial, post-Chicago man be post-literate as well? Already television has put its cool whammy on *Life.* Who'll be next? In another ten years (five years?) will anyone want to read newsmagazines? Or any other kind of magazine? Or newspapers? Or books? No one is quite sure."

Nor am I sure, in 1995, if the flinchless prophecy implied in those questions has so far turned out accurate, or is only a sample of hype-type: someone jacking off his panic button for fun and profit. The magazine isn't dead (although it's visual at the expense of verbal, increasingly); specialty titles devoted to wine connoisseurship and lesbian outing and body piercing and angelology lushly rush over the racks like paper kudzu. Nor is the newspaper comic strip dead: a 1930s classic, *Terry and the Pirates,* has just been revived (although the average strip-of-the-moment uses two-thirds less text than its earlier counterpart).

Nor is *Galaxy* dead, that far-out rocket-blasting science fiction magazine I read when I was thirteen and my eyes were alive with visions of sarong-wrapped vampish Venusians. No, not dead— but vanished, into its own predictions. It's available on-line, and on-line only. And then?—the text can be accompanied by animation sidebars. *Then?*—the animation wham!bam!zow! can be booted up and accompanied by a token bar of text. And *then?*— and then we can all be barnacles cyberwired into the imagedream machine, while the lasercode of Nuevo Rhinoceros gets piped in through the chip implants, to the minds that are malls and the malls that are brainwave networks.

Is it divine? Or is it odium? I don't know, and it isn't my place to prescribe. But I *do* know that, when family convenings at Sally's and Morrie's dragged unbearably, I'd slip off to his back room, where he'd gadgeted a ham radio for his idle play (the only ham allowed in that kosher universe), and I'd twirl its dials a while, lost in gizmory.

For a while, I would. And then I'd find myself sneaking my cousins' comic books out from under their beds—I'd dive into them and stay submerged for an hour, and I'd return with the flicker of otherworldly experience in me. Now I can see how even reading *Buck Rogers* was, primarily, *reading*—communing not with the oomph of the zowie future, but with a sensibility that, as I was learning to love it, was already slipping into the past.

Or I'd really get ambitious, and try the books on Morrie's personal shelf, woolly reminiscences from African explorers, the life of the bee, the collected Twain. A favorite was *Animal Farm*, and I relished it so—that hand-size, drably olive-green edition—that they made it a gift. I own it still, with their plate, *The Gilmans,* pasted into its front.

It would be many more years before I also read Orwell's prescient essay on the commercial and political degradations of language, but all of that was already here in *Animal Farm* as one by one the beasts of that book give up their freedoms—never having paid readerly attention to the words of their world.

✦

Last week I received a call from the marketing manager at one of my publishers. Simply: would I tape record four minutes from my forthcoming book, so she could present it persuasively to her book reps? Yes I'd do it, I grumbled. But added, "God forbid anyone should just *read.*" And then her long silence.

Look, I *don't want* to be Mr. Stuck-in-the-Mud, Sir Kvetch, some screed-empassioned crank with his mimeograph machine in the midst of the interglobal neighborhood. I don't care to bear placards and speechify. I *like* the contempo special effects in monster flicks, and caller ID on my wife's phone, and the tinny chipper voice that pipes up from some soda machines. Whatever passes for credo here, it doesn't attain the nobility of solar energy advocacy, or of William Morris's brilliantly backward-glancing attempts at medievalism.

But I know what I care to include in my days, to remain what I am, whatever that is; and I know what I need to refuse. I know this intuitively, the way we all know the quick of ourselves, the essentialness. And I'd like to be able to draw those lines of definition as hassle-free as the woman who says she's given up bourbon, the fellow who knows an adulterous liaison "isn't for me."

This essay is being written in the summer of 1995, by Bic pen in a one-dollar spiral-bound notebook. I'm going to type it on my sturdy IBM Selectramatic (electric—no manual clunker for me). And then I'll have the crew at my local Kinko's duplicate six or seven copies on paper stock 2S. And although Tomorrow may be a compelling place, and all of Dickens may fit in a fiche that's smaller than a pepper grain, and be called to the fore by voice command, and come with a 3D enhancement map of Dickens's gaslit London, and even if Dickens-simulation himself is pixeled-up to instruct me in whist . . . if it goes on a screen instead of a page, I'm sorry but the future stops *here.*

And *can* I, finally, predict that future with anything like assurance? No way. Some people's records are better than others. Wells foresaw the army tank. Twain had an inkling of television, as did a journalist, John E. Watkins, Jr., who in December 1900—with telephone only twenty-five years recent and radio nonexistent— wrote, of "the Next Hundred Years," that "persons and things of all kinds will be brought within focus of cameras connected electrically with screens at opposite ends of circuits, thousands of miles at a span. American audiences in their theatres will view upon huge curtains before them the coronations of kings in Europe or the progress of battles in the Orient. The instruments bringing these distant scenes to the very doors of people will be connected with a giant telephone apparatus transmitting each incidental sound into its appropriate place. Thus the guns of a distant battle will be heard to boom when seen to blaze, and thus the lips of a remote actor or singer will be heard to utter words or music when seen to move."

With the same astonishing accuracy, Watkins prophesied central heat and air conditioning, subway tunnels, escalators, tractors, the phonograph, even our burst of physical fitness awareness, warring submarines, "a university education . . . free to every man and woman" plus public-school free lunches for the poor, and fleets of refrigerated airplanes speeding "delicious fruits from the tropics" into Boston homes. Prognostication extraordinaire.

On the other hand (and more typically), the book *Here Comes Tomorrow! Living and Working in the Year 2000* (1966) predicts with confidence that television (improving police surveillance) will mean a drastic decline in the numbers of urban crimes, and that "despite the trend to compactness and lower costs, it seems unlikely everyone will have his own computer any time soon." Also in 1966, the *Wall Street Journal* reported this laughable gaffe of an underestimate from RCA: "By the turn of the century, there will be 220,000 computers in the United States." In thirty years, the ascendancy of the microchip has made that assessment less viable than the Code of Hammurabi.

For the most part, our piddly attempts at science fiction future-cast are much like 1950s envisionings of the Planet Patrol, its sleek-tipped rim-finned armadas of galaxycruisers, and a Space Command Center of frantically storming electrodes, all of it guided by a computer about the size of Wyoming, and then the day's statistics logged by hand in a plastic double-column entry ledger (the pen chained down so it won't float off in zero-grav)—nobody having even hazily seen the sons and daughters of silicon shrink the world and redefine its psychology.

For the most part we enter the future in bits and bytes so small, so disarmingly toe-at-a-time, we don't know it's happened until it's already a series of foregone irreversible half-decisions. One day we're us; the next, we're Pac-Man us. And the rest, as they say, is history.

But I *do* allow myself one small but fantastical, loving forecast:

In the future, on some incredibly distant planet of parallel-evolution *Homo sapiens* almost, *almost* just like us (except, of course, exquisitely advanced in matters both spiritual and tech-no), there are photoarcheologists whose calling is especially esteemed: for theirs is the labor of digging information (on a good day maybe, wisdom) out of light alone, the way *our* archeologists retrieve a splintered bone or a cusp of pottery from out of the earth and interpret it.

One day, these people unearth—or really "unlight"—a fragment of strange, oracular speech that, though it's vague in intent, is nonetheless so seemingly a verity, so manifestly summary of everything that's promiseful and terrible at once, the single sentence and its speaker attain a legendary status: the words, the face, are stored in hundreds of millions of infolockets and magnobands around the throats of these extraterrestrial citizens.

There she is, the way I remember her. *I have seen,* she says, *a dark wonder.*

Both Definitions of *Save*

Yiddish

> Hand me a relic, I'll treat it up right.
> Grandma, Grandma, rub it in schmaltz.
> Yes hand me a relic, I'll treat it up right.
> Anubis, pack it in natron salts.

Another nostalgic vignette with a grandmother canning—in this case, Nettie. It's 1960. I'm twelve. She has one year to live. You'd never guess it: her hair done up in a durable Old World bun, her hands in their finicky repetitions. Everything's sure and fluid; the gnarls and florets she's pickling in viscous brine are one with the movement that lifts and deposits them. A garnet peel of beet, an inbunched clump of cauliflower, slices, slices: cameos and medallions. She incorporates a flicked taste into her rhythm.

She hums some mouthful Old World mutter-of-a-song, and this scene is so seamlessly one piece that, finally, these twisted and whiskery vegetable nibbles can't be told apart from, *are,* the Yiddish on her tongue.

It takes her back. I'm only twelve, and maybe not the sharpest twelve at that, but I can see the wings and gutturals of her song reverse the current, take that kitchen and its passenger and soften all of their borders by fiftysome years. She touches the locket around her neck—a curl of his hair inside. She might be waiting to hear him fumble open the door, it's evening, he's home from a twelve-hour hell-day of ghetto peddling, eager to rest in her flesh . . .

I know: this has an overlush and suspect glow; I can't help it. William Kittredge says that "back deep in the misty past there is this land inhabited by dreams and passions, and you love it . . . you want it to be all perfection, bronzed in your memory like baby shoes." Canned. Sugary and canned. That's nostalgia—a marmalade.

Was she quarrelsome, ever? Did she meddle? Oh yes. Could she whine? Was she stubborn? Intuitively did she know how to slip it between the ribs and twist, and then coo guilefully for forgiveness? Of course.

But time has saved a saying from the rubble of her people: *Alleh kalles zaynen sheyn, alleh meyssim zaynen frum.*—All brides are beautiful, all the dead are holy.

Donkey pizzle! he thinks at his rival, *worm turd!* Then he burbles his heavy lips in frustration. Oh he wants this drawing by Seghers, really just a sketch not even the size of a varnish rag, but done by one of the great empassioned masters of Dutch art (now, alas, discredited in an age of taste for daintier fare than Seghers of the wild, winding lines . . .). "One hundred florins."

"One hundred and ten." Some fey young bidder, in a beaver-collared suit of bottle green, is baiting him higher by tens, and more for a lazy afternoon's game than for any understanding of the life behind the drawing. That's the prickle of it: this fellow would rather pay florins than homage.

So, "One hundred and—" Rembrandt is about to say "twenty" but why continue dancing stupid little two-step boxes with this irksome heifer? He's brought two hundred florins in his purse. The only other bidder had dropped out at eighty. "One hundred and sixty florins."

There's that half-a-breath of stillness in the warehouse. Clearly Beaver Collar is done; he fingers a wiffley dismissive gesture through the air in front of his nose, as if to say he'll be competitive, yes, but not *foolish* . . . "Well bid," the auctioneer sings on the brink of disbelief, "well bid by Master Rembrandt van Rijn of the most discerning eye . . ." and then a maundering trail of oilier compliments, as if in fear the sale might otherwise never become official.

But Rembrandt has shut off his ears. He isn't in the warehouse, and the warehouse isn't in Amsterdam or anywhere on God's Earth. There's just this one aspatial burning bridge of vision between his eyes and the drawing, he owns it, he can enter it, he could wander its charcoal lanes all day, could stretch his hand and rest it on a charcoal railing Seghers sketched, and when he lifted it off, he'd see his whole palm colored charcoal . . .

In the essay "On Collecting," Jed Perl admits and details "the grubbiness of the collector's life. Breakage, exaggerated or inaccurate descriptions, boredom, petty betrayals, overspending, regret," and of course "the terms of the marketplace."

But he also reports a small talk by Sam Wagstaff ("probably the most interesting photography collector in America"), a talk that was "a deeply serious defense of collecting, a kind of ethics of collecting. Collectors, Wagstaff argued, often labor to preserve aspects of the past—ephemeral publications, marginal works of art—when these things are headed for the trash bin, overlooked by the traditional custodians of culture. . . . Wagstaff's collector was a kind of odd man out, conservationist of the man-made past, and Wagstaff's remarks took a trajectory that made collecting seem a strangely pure, clean pursuit."

I'm not claiming this sufficiently explains each miniscule classified ad in an antiques newsletter's swatch of back pages: someone's seeking "Nazi daggers & other SS paraphernalia," someone (I'm not inventing this) is in need of "old rubber enema bags w/ nozzle, for private collection," someone "PAYING TOP DOLLAR FOR 1920'S LADIES IRON HAIR CRIMPERS!!!"

But who *wouldn't* care to dawdle in the lavishdom of that

five-story rose-brick house on Sint Antoniebreestraat? Charles L. Mee Jr. gives a sense of the wonderful jumble amassed by the later 1630s, worth quoting in full:

"Among many other things he had a little painting of a pastry cook by Adriaen Brouwer, a still life of food by Brouwer, a candlelight scene by Lievens, a moonlight scene by Lievens, a raising of Lazarus by Lievens, a hermit by Lievens, a plaster cast of two naked children, a landscape by Hercules Seghers, some small houses by Seghers, a wooded landscape by Seghers, a Tobias by Pieter Lastman, a small ox by Lastman, a portrait head by the great Raphael of Urbino, a mirror in an ebony frame, a marble wine-cooling bucket, a walnut table, a copper kettle, an embroidered tablecloth, an oak stand, some rare Venetian glass, a Chinese bowl filled with minerals, a small backgammon board, a large lump of white coral, an East Indian basket, a bird of paradise, a marble ink stand, a bin filled with thirty-three antique hand weapons and wind instruments, a bin of sixty Indian hand weapons, arrows, javelins and bows, a bin of thirteen bamboo wind instruments, a harp, a Turkish bow, seventeen hands and arms cast from life, a collection of antlers, four crossbows and footbows, five antique helmets and shields, a satyr's head with horns, a large sea plant, seven stringed instruments, a giant's head (a giant's head?), skins of both a lion and a lioness, a painting by Raphael, a book of prints by Lucas van Leyden, 'the precious book' by Andrea Mantegna, a book of prints by the elder Brueghel, a book of prints by Raphael, a book of prints by Tempesta, a book of prints by Cranach, a book with almost all the work of Titian, a book of portraits by Rubens and others, a book full of the work of Michelangelo, a book of erotica by Raphael and others, a book of Roman architecture, baskets full of prints by Rubens, Jacob Jordaens and Titian, a book of woodcuts by Albrecht Dürer, a painting by Frans Hals, a pistol, an ornamented iron shield, a cabinet full of medals, a Turkish powder horn, a collection of shells, another of coral, forty-seven specimens of land and sea animals, a Moor's head cast from life, an East Indian sewing box, several walking sticks . . ."

Now he jingles the forty florins left in his purse, and won't head home without the sea monster cleverly sewn together from the taxidermied carcasses of a monkey and a shark.

The question isn't one of ownership but stewardship—enabling separate objects, maybe even separate *moments,* to travel inviolate for a stretch, untouched by Time.

Isn't that my attempt? I'm twelve: I'm sprawled in the living room, forcing my gaze from a comic book page to watch her flurry of easy expertise at the lineup of Mason jars, half-listening to the Yiddish warble under her breath.

And: I'm forty-two, I'm looking and I'm listening back at the same.

Between these poles-of-me, a charge of preservative arcs, in which I hold her, soak her fully in it, make of her a collected thing.

The size of a saint on a dashboard: Grandma Nettie Pickling in Kitchenlight.

Held static by these various amperes and saccharines, historicized, that scene reoccurs unchanged when I want, its details clear through thirty years of episodes that otherwise grow astigmatically jagged or erode at their edges grain by grain.

The comic book is the current *Green Lantern* (No. 3, December 1960; he was my favorite superhero then, with his "power ring" and his "emerald oath": I'll tell you about him later).

Her song is a bittersweet undulation, de-DAH, de-DAH, de-de-de-DAH, oi-YOY, the last a plaintive phrase stretched thin to nearly breaking: *mein lieb, mein lieb,* my love, my love. The light is the light of late afternoon, and it denses itself in tufts of her hair that have unsprung from the bun as if a blossoming of memories are escaping her head, on fire.

In the basement below us, my father, her son, is "doing the books," as he called it, sitting hopelessly over a ledger of accounts that, opened, seemed to me to be about the size of a refrigerator, and just as cold: an oblong you could enter and have the door lock on you. Once a month, that happens to my father. He goes to take a quick look at the rent and grocery holdings, and we need to drag him out hours later, back into the land of the human.

The basement is where we've stored ill-fitting clothes and miscellaneous linens, where the dog pouts overnight, with his bowls of liverish mush and water, with his "pissy post" surrounded by fanned-out newspaper. Here, in a corner, my father positioned a desk and a thrift-shop pea-green file cabinet. This is where he comes to corrugate his forehead over the angst of household expenditure.

I know it doesn't sound pretty but, if I think of its loss, a sticky affection sludges through my system. I love the aisles in old-fashioned office supply shops. Here, I'll find similar ledgers; when I lightly run my fingers over the deep-imprinted mottling of their fake black leather covers, or when I look at the stacks of spools of paper tape of the kind he'd use in his clunker Neolithic "adding machine," punching numbers clumsily in with his forefinger, I can feel the profound emotion—the raw, familial *caring*—that kept him in place at that desk until the job was done. And I can't help but feel, gawking through some sleek new CompuCenter with its blipping "electronic money management programming/entertainment monitors" ready to forcibly cure me of a barbaric dependence on paper clips or a sentimental attachment to those docile flocks of "jumbo" erasers the pink of bubble gum . . . I can't help fear, Luddite me, that replacing the world of Frieda Garfunkle's Paper Goods & Office Notions with these très trim temples of hi-tech engineering means replacing, too, the simple generosities and ritual perseverance with which he safely saw our house through choppy fiscal waters, down there with the tape of the adding machine unspooling entry by entry into the night like a captain's log.

It's the same willful application of love I'll see through the cracked-open bathroom door when he's testing her pee for diabetes, dropping the tablet into that richly-amber vial and waiting for its alchemical play of color change—this, twice a week. Or helping her with her antiquated buttonhook shoes. (Could she be belligerent, *noodg, noodg, noodg?*—oh yes.) Or helping her, long past the days of her need for vanity, unwrap the equally antiquated iron hair crimper, heating it, curling the last sad skimplets of gray. I remember the smell of singed hair floating over her folding-bed.

Amol iz geven un haynt iz nito.— Once it was; today, no more.

The Theory of Hawthorne's Notebooks

"Something like this happens, it's crazy — then *everything's* crazy."

I'm silent at my end of the 750 miles; the phone line fills with pinprick crackles.

Craig tries clarifying his grief: "I mean, we were together *fifteen years,*" and he goes on (and on—I'm paying) to talk about missing the sharing, or helping Gaylene pack up for the move to her own apartment, "I still talk to her, do you know that?—to an empty space that follows me around." The day before, I'd phoned Gaylene. She'd said, "It hurts inside, like twigs are snapping all of the time. I'll start some smart rejoinder at a conference, and: *snap,* and then I'm just staring ahead with waterfall eyes like a loonytoon." I've known them for ten of those fifteen years, two people as snugly hinged as the wings of a diptych. Now this. It *is* crazy.

"Then," he says, "dividing up the collections!" These were the signs of their love, toy Taj Mahals by which their hearts' ineffable whoopdedo was made visible.

Miniature books (the giantmost four-postage-stamps size), each scouted out indefatigably with a strictness of passion that matched the passion that fashioned those thumbnail marbled endpapers. 1920s and '30s Mexican hand-carved carousel horses (seven, madly champing along one wall of their second-story apartment); they were chanced-on in the early days when even pinchpenny graduate students might corral these eternally fiery-maned lime and coral beauties. And (convened beneath the Big Top patiently over a decade of crosscountry hunting) one entire set of inchling Schoenhut circus figurines from three generations ago, not only the clowns, the trapezists, and dancing bears, etc., but the tents, the banners, the cages and feed troughs, the comet-painted center ring—the giraffe and the zebu, *everything*.

"Albert, listen"—I've called Craig up from a roadside telephone booth in the middle of Nowhere, Oklahoma: of course I'm going to listen—"we're nearly forty, even now we care about each other's feelings, we're civilized human beings, and there we were at four in the morning, back in the alley, howling the living piss out of our systems, fighting over the ringmaster. Over the goddam three-inch ringmaster.

"Gaylene was going to punch me one, I could read it in her musculature, but halfway there she turned it into the crack of an invisible whip, see?—*she* was the ringmaster, I was down on my knees in the glass and the burger wrappers, I was an animal being tamed, and then *I* was the ringmaster, she was on her back. . . . The only saving grace is, nobody called the police. It's *crazy*."

These are the people whose friends consult them regularly for reasoned advice. This is the couple that sleeps like spoons.

"Last night . . . I thought if only I could find *some* sensible thing to hold to, *anything*. So I looked in the newspaper." Over the roll of dustbowl wind, I hear the soft rattle of *Daily Clarion* pages, the clearing of stagey phlegm.

"'In London, a pedestrian was killed last night when an unknown assailant threw a turnip at him from a passing car. Also hospitalized was a woman who suffered severe stomach injuries after being hit by a cabbage. London police'—and it goes on."

Page-turn. "Stamford, Connecticut. 'Tattoo artist Spider Webb has opened a Bra Museum, exhibiting *100 Years of Brassieres,* including a tinfoil bra, a Plexiglas bra, and a cockroach bra.' Then he's quoted."

Page-turn. Voice is going watery now. "'A 21-year-old Phoenix woman was sentenced to jail for leaving her 18-month-old daughter locked in a closet for eight days, when' *get this*" (his voice is only the thinnest gurgle) "'she went to the hospital to have another baby . . .'

"It was all like some system for *amplifying* the craziness I was feeling. Albert, really: what kind of a cosmos *is* this?"

The answer from the start of Hawthorne's *American Notebooks* is: the cosmos is clear, and calm, and considered in partite, in language equally clear and calm.

"A walk down to the Juniper. The shore of the coves strewn with bunches of seaweed, driven in by recent winds. Eel-grass, rolled and bundled up, and entangled with it,—large marine vegetables, of an olive color, with round, slender, snake-like stalks, four or five feet long, and nearly two feet broad: these are the herbage of the deep sea."

These are the book's first words, from June of 1835; its entries continue for eighteen years, and not once is the great task flinched from: looking the world in the eye, and then finding the words for its sharpest delineation.

"The village, viewed from the top of a hill . . . It is amusing to see all the distributed property of the aristocracy and common-

ality, the various and conflicting interests of the town, the loves
and hates, compressed into a space which the eye takes in completely as the arrangement of a tea-table." That same day, he
writes of "the one-armed soap-maker, Lawyer H——, [who]
wears an iron hook," and, later, he bothers to note, "the green is
deeper in consequence of the recent rain."

He's always ready to capture Nature: sunsets, tidelines, rain-
storms, flocks and swarms, "and an enormous eel . . . truly he had
the taste of the whole river in his flesh, with a very prominent
flavor of mud." But really *all* of the things of this world are made
space for. "A withered, yellow, sodden, dead-alive looking woman,—an opium-eater." "Objects on a wharf—a huge pile of cotton bales, from a New Orleans ship, twenty or thirty feet high,
as high as a house. Barrels of molasses . . . casks of linseed oil
. . . iron in bars . . . Long Wharf is devoted to ponderous, evil-
smelling, inelegant necessities of life."

And there's another world, also accommodated. As naturally
as noting afternoon's lengthening shadows or fall's first russets,
Hawthorne writes that "the spells of witches have the power of
producing meats and viands," that "when we shall be endowed
with our spiritual bodies, I think that they will be so constituted
that we may send thoughts and feelings any distance in no time
at all." For every update on a sunrise, there's some awestruck
traipse through a landscape forever in haze, a "body possessed
by two different spirits," "a book of magic," "a phantom," "a
prophecy."

It reminds me of random paging through a huge volume of
Rembrandt's unprejudiced eye. Here, Christ preaches, backed by
an angle of sunlight as substantial as a newel post. There, a
woman brusquely raises her orchidy underskirts, to squat to piss.
The angel appears to Abraham. A rat killer peddles his service.

The many worlds are one world, finally; Hawthorne can't draw
the line. He says, "I have observed that butterflies—very broad-

winged and magnificent butterflies—frequently come on board of the salt-ship, where I am at work, where there are no flowers nor any green thing. I cannot account for them, unless they are the lovely fantasies of the mind."

I called Gaylene from a town that consisted, it seemed, of a gas pump, the pump attendant, and two thin chickens that looked as if for years they'd been used to wipe dipsticks. One half-hour down the highway, I called Craig. A man *should* worry, at the frailty of strong friends. Even their casualness disturbed me, it was something like a teapot beat out from battleship plating: its origin couldn't be hidden. Yes, I've promised them both at their separate numbers, I'll call again that afternoon, from Austin, Texas. A few minutes later, I pass an overturned crew-car of tar, which has spread to be a black circle about the size of a major resort hotel swimming pool—and even so, the landscape I'm driving through dwindles it to a demitasse serving.

I live in Wichita, Kansas, now. For ten years, though, I lived in Austin; when I left (at the end of one of those enervating bouts of post-divorce-carouse-*cum*-depression) I left near thirty cartons of miscellaneous books, old mail, and papers in Jim Magnuson's keeping, stored in the UT English Department's lock room.

"They want to make it a lounge now, buddy." And so I was coaxing the Dodge Colt south through Oklahoma, past the beckoning exit for GENE AUTRY, past the A/A rhyme scheme exit sign for the brother cities WAYNE PAYNE, through the ironed-flat plains of that state, in a bad August lull where the heat sets up shop in your marrow and deals its product from there, down memory lane, up caffeine rushes, eventually past my favorite Dallas exit sign, CAMP WISDOM RD.

I could have used some of its wares. I only vaguely remembered what dead notes and doodads were hodgepodged into those cartons, and I'd done without them smartly enough for two good Wichita years. I should have had Jim order them hauled to the dump.

Except I *couldn't* have, of course. They'd been mine and the ghosts of my fingerprints eddied, countless tiny weather maps of storms, above them yet. They'd been mine, and they called, and I hearkened. I came with fresh flat boxes and tape, to redo it all fitted to my car. Ten hours there, ten back. An idiot's errand.

I couldn't let go.

"Three-pronged steel forks . . ." "The soul . . ." What Hawthorne's notebooks do is give us such a rich collection from this olla-podidra planet of ours, the craziest elements fit. Rembrandt's oeuvre, the same.

"The thing is, you and Gaylene, your story is just one page, and you're stuck on it, reading it over and over. That's what your psyche needs to do now, read it over and over. Maybe another extraneous paragraph or three drift in from . . . a newspaper, say; but not enough to give you a sense of the whole collected *shmeer*.

"But later, a day, a year, who-knows-when, *later*—you'll read the big picture. Your own page won't seem so crazy, believe me."

Back in my divorce days, Craig would call up three, four times a night, delivering similar pep talks. So: I'm phoning him from Austin.

Louis Simpson has a poem that starts

The first time I saw a pawnshop
I thought, Sheer insanity.
A revolver lying next to a camera,
violins hanging in the air like hams

but eight lines later he's come to see the Theory of Hawthorne's Notebooks; he tells us, "Each has its place in the universe."

But Craig is little comforted by my theory, as it turns out. "Albert, listen: I want my unhappiness *over,* I don't need to hear that it has its own niche in the Scheme of Things." Well, maybe, but it was my best shot.

"Late last night I couldn't sleep, my arm kept stretching into her space in the bed, like extending it up-to-the-elbow into an alternate dimension.

"Just to take my mind off everything, I whammoed *They Saved Hitler's Brain* into the VCR. You remember."

I remember. Years ago, when I was sore in need of cheering up, we watched it: a '63 Z-level piece of schlockola that (wouldn't you know it?) by now has attracted its own "cult following."

Edited from footage shot in the Philippines (we *think*) and in America (though neither looks to have been aware, when the cameras were rolling, that it was made for wedding with the other), and with a car crash "borrowed" from *Thunder Road,* the plot is incoherent; but as I recall, a scientist's beautiful daughter and stalwart son-in-law (the love interest), somehow adventure through "Mandoras," a Latin American banana republic, saving civilized life from a band of retired Nazis who own the head of Adolf Hitler, and hatch big plans for finding *der Führer* another body and taking over the world with stockpiled canisters of nerve gas. A book on spliced-tripe cinema puts the title character's contribution this way: "Through it all, the brain of 'Mr. H.' (as he is respectfully known) is represented by a gooey, waxed face poured into a pickle jar and hooked up to bubbling, crackling, hissing life-support systems." Got it?

"Albert, get this: I wouldn't tell anyone else: but I was worn so ragged that when the dewy-eyed glances that passed for a love scene started, I began sobbing, dry sobbing, right there in my underwear. That's right, you heard me.

"Seriously sobbing."

Gaylene says: "Maybe it was 5 A.M. Did he tell you? I got the circus. Big deal. But you should see how we battled about it.

"I sat down in front of it, thinking it might help me forget. I *willed* myself, my whole self, to be just the size of my eyes. Do I have a screw loose, or what? And then I walked through the midway.

"I thought—how can I say this?—I thought I'd talk to my favorite ones. The clown with the pompom cap, who juggled oranges and tenpins. The woman who does ballet on the rump of a galloping horse. The lion tamer. I even heard the calliope music. OOMpahpah, OOMpahpah. But all of them: I'd bought them with Craig, they each had a story. Who we had to haggle with, what cobwebby corner of what slopped shop we rooted through, where we were in our lives then. Whole summers, in some cases, fish fries and walking the pier.

"It rose up from each of the figures, gradually, this foggy twin. Do you see what I'm saying? The majorette couldn't twirl her baton without this hurtful majorette-out-of-fog coming up behind her.

"And a me-of-fog, and a him-of-fog . . . Anyway," pulling herself together, "by that time it was morning. I dressed and left for work."

Hawthorne is filled with ghosts.

In groups or singly, claiming a protagonist's share of attention or simply weaving between the lines like old smoke in a pillow, black-hatted, primly bonneted, dour, they bow in sacerdotal greeting from the past, they accuse, they won't be polished off the brass like any common smudges, they mist at the window, they well up the throat and brandy won't help, they linger. On some pages, walking the streets of Concord or Salem means walking through ghosts as heavy as opera drapes.

A classically imagined one: "A ghost seen by moonlight; when the moon was out, it would shine and melt through the airy substance of the ghost, as through a cloud." What might he have done with a later, westward sensibility? Ghosts of disenfranchised Sioux and Comanche, ghosts of passenger pigeons flocking as thick as a pudding, showing visibly, as moisture on the cheeks.

In every culture there's some version of the tale where the monkey is trapped—his fist in the cookie jar, robbing it overmuch, is too full, and he can't slip out. But he won't give up even one cookie. *He* thinks it's the *jar* that won't let go.

Every ghost has a jar that keeps him here.

We see them at night, or on damp and bleary days, rain making gray twill of the air. *Let go,* they're saying, *let go of us.*

There's a promise from three generations back that needs mending; there's an unopened trunk; there's an axe; there's a locket. *Let gooooo of us.*

⋆

Language Lessons

> *Fun yidishe reyd ken men zikh nit opvashn in tsen vassern.*
> Ten waters will not cleanse you of Jewish talk.

My grandmother took an H (it meant *heart:* she'd have to be checked); they started to lead her away. The enormous receiving room was a brutal assault of confusion: clamor, tangles of lines, you didn't know for what, but ahead a woman was crying out *No, no, no,* like a child. Close to fifty immigrants sprawled in a corner in different degrees of lassitude. A girl about eight, with a shaved scalp, played with a filthy rag; you could see dull welts, from scratching, lined her cranium, as if she were some kind of medical chart.

"By the basket at the window," my grandfather said. These were his first words since they'd been sent to this line an hour before. The total of all the words he'd spoken since docking early that morning couldn't have been much more than three times that. They'd learned, on the long way over, to hold such luxuries as speech, or even obvious shows of affection, in reserve. It was a faith: that their affection wasn't dead, but in abeyance.

Now she wanted to weep at his brief and sudden Yiddish. A hunger for more of it washed through her, she wanted him shouting it at these *fershlooginer* men and women in their soiled green uniform jackets, she thought if he stopped speaking Yiddish right now, he'd be dropping the one frayed rope that still attached them at all to the world she was born in.

In 1881 Alexander III pursued what Irving Howe calls "a steady anti-Jewish policy"—this is a translation of what was often a drunk footsoldier ripping intestines out of a freshly savaged sixteen-year-old girl and waving them overhead for a trophy. "The *shtetl* began to empty a portion of its youth into the slums of Warsaw, Vilna, Lodz, Minsk, Bialystok," and, eventually, New York.

Once just a word for the hellish section belowdeck, *steerage* has come to mean, for my grandparents' people, the whole of transition experience: homeless, hungry, cut and stunned, and then the narrow oil-stained stairway down to a hard dark shelf, for being stored like sacks of coal above where the stirring-screws trembled twenty-four hours. "Someone above me vomited straight upon my head . . ." ". . . the babies throwing up even their mothers' milk . . ." ". . . in their berths in a stupor, from breathing air whose oxygen has been mostly replaced by foul gases."

The language went with. "It was the word that counted most. Yiddish culture was a culture of speech, and its God a God who spoke. . . . Neither set nor formalized, always in rapid process of growth and dissolution, Yiddish . . . acquired an international scope, borrowing freely from almost every European language . . . intimately reflecting the travail of wandering, exile."

It's not singular to the Jewish tradition, of course, that *naming* it causes it to be (in the Mayan *Popol Vuh,* for instance, "the first word" precedes "the face of the earth"). "Let there be light," and everything hierarchically follows, out of this ur-nanosecond utterance. When Adam names the animals on Eden's plains, he specifies that general creation: *kudu, dodo, cassowary, tapir, lemur, axolotl, emu, kiwi, kodiak, koala, narwhal, dog, lamb, snake,* and *angelfish.* Noah repeats this original naming at the gangplank, checking them off by twos. They're herded aboard, the crowded and terrifying journey begins, and then they're brusquely disembarked, wobbly and needing to start the world anew.

My grandparents knew this concept as the Diaspora. The clouds broke and they landed at Ellis Island. They had one paper satchel of clothes, some Yiddish proverbs, and their names.

What he meant, she understood, was "We won't leave this room until we both meet at the basket, then we'll leave together." She shook her head *no:* "Under that picture of ships." The basket might disappear, a picture hung up was a safer bet. She'd learned, the last few years, to make these swift decisions in favor of a half-degree's greater assurance. He was too worn even to wink at her savvy modification. Then, led to her line, she was lost inside another hundred just like her.

The picture was of two faintly sepia steamships, ironing out some sepia waves. He waited patiently, crumpling his hat, then carefully shaping it back again. To left and right, vast numbers of even newer arrivals were being processed. They fixed five thousand a day as the official number, but some days the truth was closer to fifteen thousand. People were being questioned, for retardation. In one room, he knew, he'd been there, a medic was lining up the men and "doing" their asses as casually and quickly as if sorting mail; he only jerked his glove in the dish of disinfectant each ninth or tenth case.

"*Oyyy . . .*" A woman, in line to have her eyelid creased back. (The eye disease trachoma caused more than half of all the medical detentions.) Where was Nettie? Women out of sight were whimpering. He tried to listen but none of the words in the air made sense, and most of what he heard as "talking" shaded off, immediately, into noise.

Now Nettie's arm was folded lightly in his, from nowhere it seemed, from out of the barracks dinge, and by her face he knew she'd passed whatever arcane cardiac gauntlet was required.

Without a word, they walked to the outside rail and breathed New York over the water. She looked back: of course, the basket was gone. Did she have the right wall?—even the sepia ships had disappeared.

They were off: the hawsers whipped up, the ferry bucked. What did he see, with his okayed eyes and his okayed wife beside him? Not much, fog was low; you couldn't see three feet ahead. The harbor reeked, and the ferry chopped through it with equal pungency: feta cheese in splotchy wheels, old mattress ticking, sausage in hog-bowel casings, tins of greasy feathers, sheaves of leather, wrinkled dried fruits knotted up in a kerchief, babies' bottomrags.

They docked. Somewhere he'd lost his hat. The dockworkers' voices, more strange than the gulls'.

Then they were at "the Pig Market," Hester near Ludlow. The streets were . . . you see? They didn't have the words.

A welter of pushcarts sorted the little late-afternoon light: peaches a penny a quart, alarm clocks, cucumbers floating in milk tubs, watch it buddy, faster, kapow, by the hundred, whores, look move it, wagons hauling the Christian proselytizers, a boy not over twelve distributing cards with the whores' addresses, neckties straightened just *so,* that's my place mac, cracked eggs, the boxing match this, hey sugar, the boxing match that, beneath these new American angels: pigeons, gray and mean.

Says Irving Howe, "The density of the Tenth Ward . . . shortly after the turn of the century was greater than most of the worst sections of Bombay." And, "The first English expressions that struck my foreign ear as I walked through the ghetto that day . . . were 'sharrap' (shut up) and 'garrarrehere' (get out of here). It took me a little while to learn that the English tongue was not restricted to these two terms."

They rested near the scissors man, his grindstone throwing off sparks. Nettie sat on their single satchel. She wished he hadn't lost his hat, the way his hair was thinning. She knew how he could be about that. *Draikop,* she told herself, "silly head." How *much* had they lost, this last year, and here she was worrying over a hat.

"They gots some help for greenhorns." He'd put down a scissors to motion across the street, then he repeated his statement in Yiddish—a *landsman!* Was she *tzedráyt,* insane? She wanted to reach at his lips and catch it all leaving, as if they might be tiny birds.

"They'll get us rooms? A job?" My grandfather knew of such agencies, even had some names folded into his pocket; still, in the midst of the tumult, this news appeared incredible.

"Sure. Now, please . . ." (switch to English) "I dunt gots da time." And back to the turning wheel.

That evening, as boarders in a tenement flat, they each unscrewed a door and set it on two low fish-smelling crates, and so had side-by-side beds in a room where four other people already snored. The room was dim, but she could see one sleeper's upturned cheek was fissured with scars; they were thin, as if maybe a knife. My grandfather tied a string from his leg to the satchel.

Whispering.

"What's Sarah doing back home, do you think?"

He thought. "I don't know." Silence. "This is our home."

"It was some day, yah?"

"Yes. This ice with the flavor in, it was good."

"But still, it was some day."

"Yes."

"Sarah must be closing up the shop by now, with the new goods."

"I said I don't know."

"I only . . ."

Harsh: "I-said-I-don't-know."

(Already the trouble was starting. In that dim room you could still see it coming.)

Silence.

Then, making light of his ire: "Ah, why don't I sharrap."

They held hands, slab to slab. When it was clear that their roommates would sleep through a *pogrom,* he slurred her a lullabye in his late-night after-some-vodka voice of the old days, *Netteleh, Netteleh, zing mir a lideleh,* tracing tightening circles over her breasts. But he fell into sleep the first, a weary man on the fidgeting end of a string.

She couldn't sleep, there was this plank inside her as stiff as the door beneath. She walked the two flights down to the stoop, too weary herself to feel caution. For a while she only stared with passive fixity at the scraps of moving moonlight on a trickle of filth in the gutter across the way. She started singing then, a childhood tune in a lighthearted hush, *Mama makes with the tea for me, Papa makes with the honey, When I grow up I'll dance all day, And buy white lace with my money.*

A street dog trotted up and forthrightly rested its head in her lap. It was ragged and, from what she could tell in the half-dark, seemed to be the color of a wen. She stroked its snout.

"Dat's a pretty song, lady."

"Yah, yah, pretty. Pretty-schmitty. From a long time back."

"Dun't be so cynical, kiddo. A voice like yours, like a lark on da ving, troo' da fields—*hoo!* You could rule dis crapped-up vorld."

"So show me this lark. So show me this field, Mr. Big Shot Dog."

"Vell . . . howzabout I show you da crapped-up world part? I gots mit plenty of dat."

"From that, I don't need seeing no more."

"Oh, like it or not, you gonna, *tsahtskaleh.* Up and down, morn to moon, vork and a liddle more vork. May as vell face it down mit your tail up, dat's vhat us dogs say. Look, I come by sometime, I show you around."

"Yah, sure, why not?"

"Mr. Loner Dog, Mr. Boner Dog, Mr. Howler mit Growler mit Groaner Dog—dat's me. You'll *zing* me some more? A *lideleh?*"

"Yah, yah."

"Okay by me. So tell me: you ain't puzzled, a dog should be talking like dis here to you?"

"First, *hoont,* you're a dream. The second, you make me more sense in my head than any talk yet in America."

"Fletterer. Go back now. Go, sleep by him."

"Yah, sleep . . ."

sleep . . . .

(joking:) "Garrarrahere."

It was a mongrel.

It razzed the fatcat boys, it blatted out its ass, it danced in circles with God for a partner, it boozed and it shmoozed and it prayed all night in the coal cellar under the buttery light of a few thumbs of tallow—this Yiddish.

It resourcefully lopes into History, from the basin of the Moselle and the banks of the Rhine, around 1100, a quadruhybrid: Rabbinic Hebrew, Old French, Old Italian, and Middle High German, a language in search of a saint and an all-night poker game, this Yiddish, this mongrel, this backstreet patchwork creature, suspect, coupling in the alley crannies, thieving, lean and wry and rolling a phlegm in its throat as rich as spermwhale oil. Somewhere in between the blazing gates of heaven and the backstage door of a burleyque joint, its *oy* and *ich* are bickering, dickering, giving a *yoohoo* out the window, scented with a breathy mishmash of lox and *kasha* and stomach bile.

Over five hundred Yiddish words have officially crossed into *Webster's.* From the earliest days, the New York ghetto was home to a flexible "Yinglish." Say one affluent week you scrounge an extra nickel or two, you saunter to the soda parlor. Restauranting, foreign to a *shtetl* Jew, "is spreading every day," the *Jewish*

Forward reported in 1903. You take the missus's arm, you go for a double dip: *oysesn,* "out-eating."

But language lags. The trolleys swoosh their first fierce time before your greenhorn eyes, with the confusing force of Ezekiel's roil of wheels, and the words for it don't catch up for a while.

Our sense of the future *requires* that wait, Bronowski says. Once input flashes whambang into the brain, it enters a period of "reflection, during which different lines of action are played through and tested." Memory, which Bronowski defines as "the storing of signals in some symbolic form, so that they may be used to revive our senses in the future," is possible only "if the initial response . . . is delayed long enough to separate some abstract marker and fix it in the brain. This is basically a linguistic mechanism."

In this way, language and memory enable—in some sense, even may be—each other. William Gass: "I remember—I contain a past—partly because my friends and family allow me to repeat and polish my tales." In a Louis Simpson poem, "Profession of Faith," the speaker understands that a memory of his wife "in the garden . . . reaching up, pulling a branch," and of a purely fictional figure spectrally "floating in midair," really are equivalent:

> The things we see and the things we imagine,
> afterwards, when you think about them,
> are equally composed of words.
>
> It is the words we use, finally,
> that matter, if anything does.

Gass again: "To *know* is to possess words . . . we name incessantly, conserving achievements and customs, and countries that no longer exist."

She stands in the kitchen, preserving. Light goes sea-green in the Mason jars, the smell of brine pinches the air. Or she's not there at all, no, she's humming her Yiddish ditties and it's 1911, her hair is an inky plait to her waist, his lips are idly jittering over the small of her back as she's singing for him, a low, slow, soulful version of a village tune they'd do together reining the wagon up to its rail at Sarah's shop for tannery goods, and then she'd invite them for sweet tea, with the samovar winking the lees of the sun off its sloped copper shoulders, an heirloom, she insisted, from the grandmother she most missed . . .

conserving countries that no longer exist

✦

Bundles

They paid for a one-room apartment by now, a crate that nightly floated them over the *dreck* and commotion. Both of them worked, though hers was part-time seamstressing for a shopfront two or three removes from the garment district's major mayhem. And, in slack times, she could bring her baskets of rough cloth home: they'd play that she was a lady of leisure.

"Shit!" She'd pricked her thumb. She didn't so much learn the word, as have it simply seep into her from the streets, an ineradicable brown dye streaking her standard lessonbook English. He tried to, but couldn't, drum home its difference from her other, native imprecation, "Feh!" and in time it replaced the earlier word completely. Once, when they were having an argument: "Can it!" she blurted, no less surprised than he was, "Baloney!"

But nothing stopped Mr. *Hoont* from visiting. Loneliness could summon him, or wearying toil; she suffered both, and through her hazed half-wakefulness, he'd gradually materialize, always with a harmless leer or with made-up news from the Old Country: Yasha was doing this now, Sarah that. At these times, English shinnied out the room's one window and down the drainpipe. Yiddish filled the room then, every sentence like a burning-red bouquet set into a milk glass vase, until the space around her was roses and fire.

And my grandfather?—he had his own companion, not a dog, a

dybbuk, a spirit, a streetwise guy in a slanting derby. Anyway, that's what the voice was like. It hovered outside the window some nights while she was asleep, it hovered there as if on a cloud of streetstink-and-squabble. *Forget the pack,* it told him. *You can leave it all behind you, guy. It's easy, just trust me. Let gooooo of it...*

About the pack:

"In the cities of the North," says Howe, "during the years of industrial expansion, peddling was backbreaking and soul-destroying work." He quotes Morris Witcowsky, on his merchandise pack: "Weighed about a hundred and twenty pounds, eighty pounds strapped to the back and a forty-pound 'balancer' in the front." Then you walked, you climbed, the tenement stairs of the ghetto blurring to one enormous treadmill. Knock. Who is it? DryYYY GooOOOoods. Get out of here you show your hooknose face again I'll kick your ass clear back to Roosia. Twelve hours a day of this, until at the end the pack was the brain, the rider, and you were its well-whipped beast.

"You want a *bisseleh* ice cream?" he asked her.

"No, but I come with." She set down the sewing—a yellow strip of buttonholes in a basket of strips of buttonholes. "Maybe just for the air, yes? Some fresh air."

He was silent.

The light in their single room was often lost halfway to the floor, so giving it the thick look of an aquarium of ill-kept water. Even with the window opened, the feeling was often one of uncut murk.

"It would be nice, the fresh air."

"I *heard* you, Nettie!" He spoke, though, in the direction of the pack. It filled one corner. There was a night when she woke, he was snoring exhausted beside her, and she thought she saw it twitch in the gloom, then grow in front of her eyes.

Too much was new, "the way people walked, the rhythms of the streets, the division of the day into strict units of time, the disposal of waste, the relations among members of the family, the exchange of goods and money." And Howe continues, "That symptoms of social dislocation and even pathology should have appeared under the extreme circumstances in which the early Jewish immigrants lived, seems unavoidable."

Gangs were common, especially gangs of pickpockets, "grifters," and up to 30 percent of all delinquents brought before the Children's Court of New York in 1906 were Jewish. On some streets—Allen, Rivington, Stanton, Delancey—prostitution flourished. "Dancing academies" trained young girls and recruited pimps, "cadets." The Yiddish term for "whore," of course, a *nahfkie* or a *koorveh,* long preceded the wave to America; and still, for some, it's surprising to see such obviously Jewish names appearing on lists of offenders: "Lena Blum, Ida Katz, Sadie Feldman . . ." They squatted on stoops, exhibited thighs that bulged like overripe bries. Some knitted, some chewed Russian sunflower seeds; they squeezed their breasts with rude duck honkings. And here, the famous hoodlums—Legs Diamond, Little Kishky, Spanish Johnny, all Jews—concocted their apprenticeship swindles.

Husbands abandoned their families. Pressures and temptations were extraordinary, after all. Of requests for financial relief made to United Hebrew Charities in 1903 and 1904, 10 to 15 percent came from deserted women; by 1911, a National Desertion Bureau had been established. For years, the most popular features of the Yiddish newspaper the *Forward* were the "Bintel Brief" (the "Bundle of Letters"), where readers wrote in with their crises, and the "Gallery of Missing Husbands," where, as a typical instance, Bessie Cohen would be "looking for Nathan Cohen my husband, an umbrella peddler, 22 years old, the little finger of his right hand is bent. He abandoned me and a five-month-old baby in great need. I offer $25."

The *dybbuk* was busy. *Let gooooo of it . . .*

The air down in the streets *was* fresher, marginally. The great machine-tinged winds of the elevated's passing clatter quivered those dense heated blocks of aroma that rested above their designate pushcarts: fish spillings, hardening butter, mushbodied cabbages. A broomstick-and-tincan game of baseball hogged one corner. On Allen Street, the girls yoohoo'ed and flashed their ankles in playful scissoring kicks.

"No, Nettie. We go down some other way."

"Yes, hokay." She'd been distracted by the ragtag game of ball, the ganglier older players, and one befuddled six-or-seven-year-old who was waddling about with a sopping pantsfull—for a while now, she'd been thinking of children. But then: "Oh, wait. It's Lena. *Leeena!*"

"Nettie." A tug. His hand like a mastiff at her black sleeve.

"Wait, it's Lena. Lena!"

Halfway down Allen, Lena crossed her meaty calves and waved back.

"You know such a woman?" The pack had been heavy all day with a thousand weights, and now this.

"This is Lena," she said, beginning to sense the enormity of the situation, what she'd started in crossing a social boundary for companionship's sake, her English beginning to stumble under the stress, "from Cracow. *Nu?* She *geb* me butter, to her I *geb* salt." Something in his look. "She makes my friend." You traded butter for salt, back then, and there, it made you a friend. Prouder in repetition, and as if the naked fact of it undid a net of lesser considerations, "She makes my friend."

This extra weight, this thousandth-and-one. He felt his eyes grime over with some emotion he had no word for, not in any of his languages.

"Come Nettie. We go now." The el rattled past; this close, they both could feel shiverings inside their bodies like dishes and ewers precariously shelved.

"We go down Allen Street, yes? It would be short. To say hello Lena. Salt I give her, is all. For the pickled herring."

"You do not know such women."

"I have eyes, I see things. *You* know such women."

Then he called her a name.

In the wake of the el, the silence became like a third party standing there with them.

"I think you go back, for the pack," she said. "In it you put your clothes and your *chuchik* for the cigarettes and your knife." She paused. "You will not no more live inside my house." She'd never before said anything so softly, and by this he knew its sincerity.

He was gone that night.

She stepped in the space where the pack had been. Its absence ordered the room around it, as definitely as its presence had. "Shit! Shit!" and she pulled her hair. Then she fell to the floor, and was weeping into her basket of cloths, she wept now for the first time since he'd shouldered his belongings and stepped through the door. Her eyes poured it lavishly out, she imagined the basket spilling it onto the boards. Her last thought, right before sleep: that Lena could come for this bundle of salt now, could borrow as much as she wanted.

The monster came flying.

It missed his head by inches, unstitching apart in mid-air, the shark half falling gracelessly into a puddle on the after-rain clay, but the monkey half continuing in a high arc, with its stuffing showering out of its undone bottom, and a swag of dirty linen trailing out of the same, snapping like a pennant.

"No! And no! And no!" Hendrickje was screaming at him from where she stood in the doorway, each deep-throated *no* volleyed into the lane with the angry strength she'd given to pitching the curio.

Rembrandt shuffled there, speechless, angry in turn (the two hundred florins was *his* commission, not hers) and shamed (but wasn't it true she'd been counting each carrot these days, each seam in a hem, and what could he expect when she returned from the market with fishtails for the broth because anything savorier was beyond their meager means this week, and waiting for her in the hush of the parlor, on a teak base, was Mathilde, as he'd taken to calling his purchase, Mathilde wearing an overturned tulip on her head to crown her "Queen of the Deep" . . .) and then angry again, no not at Hendrickje posing with her hands on her aproned hips in classic pique, and not with himself, but simply with circumstance, that had brought them together, and then had brought them to this. He gingerly lifted the shark-half, shrugged at its lumpishness, sighed once (histrionically: she was watching, still), then turned and shambled off. He'd snugged Mathilde's wet netherpart under one arm, and a sketchbook under the other.

Somewhere in between the house on the Rozengracht (for this is where he lived now, having lost the earlier showplace-of-a-dwelling) and the synagogue (for that was his destination) he let go the ratty remnant of shark; he couldn't even remember where or how.

But the sketchbook he gripped as if it would float him over these recently troubled waters. The sketchbook was where he would stay for the afternoon, until he was healed of ire and guilt. He eased himself up to the shadow-side of a pillar (they didn't all like being sketched, these Sons of David), unwrapped a stick of charcoal, and let the nimbleness that lived in his fingers run free. "Going Jewing," a neighbor of his had derisively termed it. All right then, he was. The faces here were creased and hurt and determined in ways he'd never seen in any other Amsterdam face, though sometimes they reminded him, crazily enough, of an unworldly gaunt-cheeked bearded look he'd seen in certain fish at the market he privately thought of as "High Priest fish."

"No other Amsterdam painter did as many portraits of Jews as Rembrandt. One scholar has guessed that about a fifth of Rembrandt's portraits of men are Jews—this at a time when the Jews represented perhaps one percent of the population of Amsterdam.

This would fit with the general impression that Rembrandt gives of a temperament moved more by personal warmth than by ideology" (Charles L. Mee Jr.).

Some of his friends were Sephardic Jews, educated, assimilated denizens of the cultural life. But today, at the synagogue, Rembrandt is sketching furiously at the faces of Ashkenazim, newly arrived from Poland: the women in shawls and slipping wigs, the men in tunics concocted of grain sacks tied by rope at the waist, and their faces!—inward-looking, ethereal, and yet tuber-like faces! One is cantankering with a compatriot now, and he places a finger alongside his nose, for every point of logic he scores . . .

Because I'm trying to write of how and why we save things over time, I'll quote what Kenneth Clark says, "He had always loved painting Jews: he saw in them repositories of ancient wisdom and an unchanging faith."

. . . and almost as quickly, a finger in charcoal takes shape alongside a charcoal nose.

⁺

Zamlers

"Because I'm trying to write of how and why we save things over time," I wrote, and meant both definitions of *save:* "to collect" and "to rescue."

"The word for it is *hemshekh,*" Aaron Lansky says, "'continuity.'" Lansky sweeps an open hand at seven hundred thousand Yiddish-language books on the floor of a renovated paper factory in Holyoke, Massachusetts; there are two hundred thousand more in the National Yiddish Book Center's primary office, and six or seven hundred donated volumes a week are still received. "This is from the world Hitler tried to destroy."

In 1980, when Lansky was twenty-four, he founded the Center with earnings from a summer of migrant blueberry picking in Maine. The Center consisted of a government-surplus typewriter and a picnic table. Ten years later, Lansky heads a network of a hundred volunteer *zamlers* ("collectors") and eight thousand dues-paying members. Not all of the titles are warehoused; some already have "been returned to circulation, restored to the life of books" for readers in Brooklyn, Thailand, Guam, or Tokyo. "As native speakers pass on, the books become the sole access to the last thousand years of Jewish history."

It's as if he lives in a sentence, at exactly the inky atom of a sentence, where the word *razed* puns into *raised*. "They're giving up a library," Lansky says of his typical elderly Jewish donors; for them "it's like a moment of transition.

"They're giving up the library before they die. So they often cry and tell stories."

Time loves a book—to fox its pages in lovely rust, tea, sepia, and fecal starclusters; to brittle it; to riddle it with pin-width insect labyrinths; to fade, chip, buckle, cockle, scrape, and in general tick eternity away by units of wholesale decomposition; Time loves to suck a book as clean as a chicken wingbone.

A. D. Baynes-Cope's *Caring for Books and Documents* reads like the opening speech of a five-star general to his troops in time of war. He is stern and exact, and his epaulettes flash like artillery in the parade ground sun, as he tells his ranks, "We know what books and documents are made of, and how these materials can be expected to behave in various climactic conditions, what their enemies are and how to outwit them." The foe is legion. "Light is an enemy of books. . . . Heat can also be an enemy of books. . . . Indirectly windows are an enemy of books. . . . Fire and flood are obviously major enemies." The ugly truth is, "every solid, liquid or gaseous object in this universe is a chemical or a mixture of chemicals," and so of course is suspect of constant attack.

Cats are enemies, and the fleas on the cats are enemies, and the microbes on the fleas are eager to swirl across a library's spines in garish fungal sargassos. "Indeed, the enemies may be internal"— a book's own traitorous acids can eat it into oblivion, like a man's heart's being lapped by that man's own bile. Need it even be said that "we can include human beings as an enemy of books through sins of omission and commission"?

There is no question but that the war must be fought. But Baynes-Cope refuses to euphemize the privations that await us: "Time, thought, trouble and money must be expended." For instance, if insect damage is merely hinted at, "the treatment must be designed to cope with the likelihood that all four stages of insect growth—egg, larva, pupa and insect—are present. Even if only one book is affected, those books on that shelf, and the ones above, below, and backing onto it, must be examined thoroughly, preferably out of doors, and the infected books brushed with a soft paint-brush or gently with a vacuum cleaner fitted with a softish baluster brush"; the latter "is a little fierce but the suck can be reduced by drilling a few ¼ or ⅜ in (6mm or 9mm) holes in the tubing." Bats require yet greater effort. Sniffing for dampness earns its own dense paragraph of instruction. Never let the size of the battlefront mislead you into underestimating the toil required: "The problems of producing a safe climate in a single case may be more difficult than those for a single room."

Is it worth it, this endless seriocomic operatic clash of the forces of Entropy and Conservation? The answer is wholly serious. Aaron Lansky recounts his first book-gathering mission, to an eighty-seven-year-old man named Temmelman, in Atlantic City: Lansky arrives at noon, to find the man in his apartment building's lobby. "I hope you haven't been waiting long." "Oh I been here since 7 this morning, young man. I diddin want I should miss you."

Every volume has its history. "You know, my wife and I . . . this book we bought in 1925, yes! We went without lunch for a week we should be able to afford it."

Everybody's saving, from cereal boxtops to souls.

Imagine standing in the restorer's lab as the first dabbed fraction of night in "The Night Watch" cleans back into the patchily almondine daylight of Rembrandt's palette. Banning Cocq, Van Ruytenburgh, Vischer, Engelen, Kemp, and the rest of the musketeers are gridded-*n*th-of-an-inch-by-*n*th revisioned, as the very molecular bonding of midnight breaks, swabs off, and clears the fine-crazed stage for an intricate play of the effects of sun on their faces and antique costumery. That room must have been an enormous held breath.

Reviving hither, regilding yon, the World Monuments Fund is endlessly busy—fifty restoration projects in fifteen countries. Sculpture on the portal of the Collegiate Church in Toro, Spain . . . Diego Rivera murals in Mexico City . . . Easter Island . . . Angkor Wat . . . One current project is the Château de Commarque, which sits on a cave of wall engravings and paintings twenty thousand years old: a leaping horse, a profiled human head, and so many obvious male and female symbols that prehistorians call the cave "the sex shop." Hubert de Commarque: "Our lives are a bit lost today because we have lost the knowledge of the earth, of the sky. . . . That is what I want most from this work—to give to the people that connection that's been lost."

For some, the glory days of burlesque—the legendary plumed glitterqueens and their retinues. For some, the lone orchid pressed in an album; its oils have long past stained the paper around it translucent, a wimple of spectral sheen.

"It's history. It's art. It's culture. It's dying." On page 24 of this issue of *Amtrak Express,* the Lighthouse Preservation Society asks for your help to "Keep It Shining." Page 9, the Save the Manatee Club suggests you "ask about our 'Adopt a Manatee' program." Who *wouldn't* want to halt their extinction? Seal-bodied hippos is what they look like, a ton of sea-grass-munching rotundity. Only twelve hundred or so remain in U.S. waters. The California condor needs saving, and our culture may never again see the like of the smokily peignor-petaled bodies of 1940s Vargas-style pinup art. Fountain pens. Cuspidors. Bauhaus.

Someone's brushing crumbs of dirt from between two tiny marble toes. That's all: two tiny marble toes, unattached to anything. The brush is correspondingly tiny, and softer than a cosmetician's rouge brush. What is it about the Past? We're down on our knees at two of its toes, and it's beautiful, the way the veins in the marble simulate veins in the flesh. Send in your money. Help save the toes. They'll be photographed, labeled, and wrapped in seven layers of cotton and styrofoam sheeting. Somewhere: marble legs and a torso (where, though?). Somewhere: marble wings.

Angels. Since 1976, Joyce Berg has collected 8,366 figurines of angels. One sits with its legs crossed, reading a book, and looks like a seven-year-old on the potty. A somberly religious one raises its fingers in ritual benediction. Angels in crystal, in wood, in ceramic. One, in clay, is carrying a halo on its head like a balanced doughnut. One is clearly a cat, in a celadon ballerina's getup. Lowell Berg says, "She writes down where she bought it, when, what she paid, whether the clerk was bald; you know, all the important stuff."

George Logue owns fifty working two-ton Caterpillar tractors (including—his most prized—a 1932 diesel model), arranged like a pasturing herd, on his family farm. Ken Soderbeck: a dozen antique fire trucks (including the 1912 Knox piston pumper) with subsidiary uniforms, equipment, and Tisch and Ike, his two dalmations. Tom Bates: thirty thousand soda and beer cans, amassed in his and his sister Ginnie's Museum of Beverage Containers and Advertising. Jim Hambrick: wowee! an assemblage of Superman figures, banks, comic books, board games, pinbacks, clocks, etc., forty thousand superitems large.

Whenever I'm glum these days, I go to this photo in which Bab Malkin sits amid the icons of his passion. "It's all I thought about. I'd go to flea markets before dawn with a flashlight." He collects giantdom—oversize advertising memorabilia. Here, he's perched in a chair that diminishes him to a two-year-old's size, though a two-year-old in a business suit and tie. One foot rests on top of a shoe (a natty wingtip brogue) with the bulk of a motor scooter; the other foot's in a gym shoe you could coddle a papoose inside of spaciously. There's a birdbath-diametered coffee cup, a pocket watch like one of a sixteen-wheeler's tires, a telephone you could straddle for a carnival ride, and Malkin's wearing this silly grin sized perfectly for his face, and signing a legal pad, roughly of loveseat length, with the Fountain Pen of the Gods.

"Pull in here." And doughty Kit Hathaway did—a comic book shop we were passing by chance in Saratoga. I was his guest for two days surrounding a reading I gave at Union College and, stout heart, he was striving mightily to cater to my trashorama needs. You never know what you'll find in a back bin of yellowing paper. Not Kit, not two customers browsing t-shirts, or the clerk heard the clarion blasting through my cochlea. But there it was, from thirty years back, exactly as I remembered: *Green Lantern* No. 3, December 1960.

As you may know, Green Lantern is "really" Hal Jordan, test pilot for the Ferris Aircraft Company in Coast City. One day, a trainer plane he was testing lifted into the air mysteriously, and was guided to where a spaceship lay crashed in the desert. Summoned inside, Hal met the dying extraterrestrial Abin Sur (bald, angle-browed, and jellybean-red), who with his final words decreed Hal Jordan his successor as this sector-of-the-universe's "Green Lantern." He had the costume prepared, and the power ring, and he taught Hal Jordan the sacred Oath Against Evil that must be recited when recharging the ring at the Power Lamp every twenty-four hours. Through the ring, green psychic energy made the leap to solidity, and many is the ne'er-do-well who found himself, in the midst, say, of a bank heist, lifted by limousine-sized green tongs, then slammed by a man-high green hand efficiently into a green cage, and then whisked on a flying green platter straight to the calaboose. The Oath was stirring:

> In brightest day, in blackest night,
> No evil shall escape my sight!
> Let those who worship evil's might
> Beware my power, Green Lantern's light!

That's the genesis story I must be referring to here, in *GL* No. 3, on page 2 of "Green Lantern's Mail Chute": *Dear Editor: I think Green Lantern is one of the most exciting and different action magazines on the market today. However, I was disappointed when half of the exciting lead story, "Planet of Doomed Men," was devoted to Green Lantern's origin, which already had been printed in the first issue. Albert Goldbarth, Chicago Ill.*

I plunked down thirty dollars for what was once a ten-cent comic book, and left the shop whistling.

My First Published Work.

> it is not what a thing is
> but what you feel about it that counts.
> —Louis Simpson

I'm twelve, I look up from reading that page—or I look up from my writing about my reading that page, it really doesn't matter—and see her working in light the kitchen curtains texture. Fussing at all of those jars mechanically. Her mind in a circle of othertime.

And when I see my father, in this same replaying retrospective scene, he's always down at that desk, embattled by numbers, the spiral of tape from the adding machine having frozen his pose, and me, and Grandma Nettie, and by extension every mote of 1960—like a watchspring having frozen the hands of its watch, or like the coiled soul of a wind-up toy having frozen its colorful body into a single gesture forever.

In that block of stalled chronology, she's stopped to touch the locket at her throat. The counter is rowed with crocks of cucumbers canopically floating. I see it as if a bolt of green power has leaped from between my hands and, charged with all of the voltage of human wishing, has zapped this picture permanent. Lascaux won't fade, Hal Jordan won't fail, the diabetes won't eat her away.

✦

Kishef for the Swigman

In six months he hadn't uttered a word of Yiddish. And the words he'd learned—! A clown is a "joey." A fistfight with the locals is a "clem." Here he'd learned "cunt," and that his cigarettes were "coffin nails." He was called a "razorback" or "roustabout"— he'd help the elephant push their handful of gaudy, gewgawed wagons out of backroads mire. Godiva said he could work up to joey one day, but when? Godiva in her bareback rider's flouncing tutu. Godiva was a "star."

"Hey, mac": it had happened this simply. "Think you can handle a hammer?" So he'd pitched in, on that first day nearly half-a-year back, as they hoisted the canvas, guying-out its violently flapping sides. It was a sixteen-pound sledgehammer—it was, as he'd learn to say here, "no picnic"—but, as he sweated his *kishkes* out, he sweated out everything bitter inside, that horseradish taste on his tongue, he sweated away the last dust of the pack and its prisoning ghetto world: he couldn't have been farther away, here with The Human Cannonball, and Mad Marie the Mule-Faced Girl, and the uric tang from the one sad tiger's groin-shag weaving around its wagon as palpably as the one sad anaconda might.

"Your name?" the ringmaster had asked. And he'd said *"Vhat?"* in his accented English in response, not expecting the question, and intuiting immediately that a new life required a new appellation, that he would need to keep a line between the two people he was, and yet he hadn't had the time to think this over. "Walt?" said the ringmaster, "Walter?" So he'd been put on the payroll that way. *Walter* was entered alongside Barko the Ape Man, and Lisette, and Hi-Step Hank, and Wonder-o.

And there was Godiva. Her hair was gold and ringleted, as perfect as torquing in some machine. She shamelessly worked her butt when she walked. He'd seen her bend with her ass in the air, a spangled tutu framing it; she'd uncork a bottle of wine between her knees. His first day there, she threw him the look. But he was careful. He was new, a Jew to boot, and far from home. He hadn't imagined it, though—the second day, a look. One night he drank too much, When? he asked her. He even fell to his knees. Not yet, she told him. She fingered a ringlet. Later, when he'd proved himself, when he moved up in rank and they made him a joey. This was probably true, he reasoned. There were three clowns and she granted her favors to two of them. (The other was Mad Marie's.)

For now, his primary duty was catering to Professor Oink the Educated Pig. A pig!—if he wanted to turn from the world of the rabbis, he'd certainly managed. He also hauled the wagons, as I said, and watered Jumbo, and did a bit of whatever ball-busting and ego-eroding drifter's labor was required. But lately Professor Oink, who added, subtracted, and told the future, was a special draw, and so was provided with special attention.

My grandfather brushed him and hand-fed him cabbage and just before showtime wiped the shit he'd been rolling in, from his flanks and rump. It never failed: every showtime, shit. A few weeks into this assignment, and it was the moment he thought of his wife most tenderly. *Shit, shit, shit,* he heard her clumsily saying, and smiled. He thought of her often. He sent money every week, no note but money (all he earned, in fact). She'd be seamstressing, he knew. He felt the needle in his heart.

But always, Godiva was there. And always, something new was happening. Sheriffs were running them out of the county. Hellfire preachers, with burning crosses and monkeys dressed up like devils, would join forces with them for a town or two. The tiger, Bengali, escaped once and they found him on top of a wagon of hay bales, terrified: a yapping dog about the size of a handkerchief was streaking around the wheels. It was a shabby excuse of a circus; the one-time parakeet-green of its handbills and banners had faded to a color that looked coughed up. But they attracted crowds, in back-bend towns where funerals and shotgun weddings were usually the only diversion. One day, flies and itch and nothing else. The next day, TOOT-TOOT-TOOT, hey, the circus!

And he had a plan. He was learning magic. Canchak the Great had quit the show, in Salliesburg. The story included the mayor, the mayor's wife, and the circus's dancing bear, and no one agreed on the details, but the following morning the bear and the mayor remained, while the other two featured participants disappeared into the moonlight.

No matter: now there was clearly an opening. He practiced in secret. The day was hot, and everybody else was sprawled in the relative cool of the wagons. He was sitting in the shade of a stunted maple, alongside Professor Oink. Tell me, pig, pick a card. Okay, now wait, you see here? Look—*your card!* But Oink, from a line of professionals, was singularly unimpressed.

And Nettie?

She didn't need him. She could buy her grapneled chicken legs without his help, she'd even finagled a new (used) feather mattress. Once a week the envelopes arrived in care of the Jewish Women's Organization, and every week she slipped the twelve dollars into a celluloid whatnot box, refusing to spend it, to be so demeaned—and with the emptied envelopes she lined the birdcage. *Pisher'l,* that was the bird: Little Pisser.

"*Nu?* He's a bum, a no-goodnik."

"Yah, yah, Lena."

"*Yah* you say, but you don't *listen*. He's a bum, *a shandel un a charpeh*." A shame and disgrace. "Now you say it."

"Lena . . ."

My grandmother chopped in the kitchen—or what saved space in the room, by the red-and-white-check oilcloth's declaration, became the "kitchen." He'd been gone six months and she'd moved, though leaving a message behind, with the new address. She was happy here, some days she hummed to the onions, *mein lieb, mein lieb;* once Lena unexpectedly knocked, and found her dancing in circles, with a shirtwaist from her basket of work. This new room had sun; it filled the window, making gilded Russian domes of the onions. In one corner Pisher'l, himself the shape of a gold note, sang and dipped to his dish of gold seeds.

Irving Howe: "Never having regarded herself as part of a spiritual elite, she did not suffer so wrenching a drop in status and self-regard as her husband. She was a practical person, she had mouths to feed, and, by and large, she saw to it that they were fed."

And "large" is the word. At night, without the sun, and while Pisher'l balled up into sleep, she wept—she rubbed her burgeoning tummy, slowly, singing, *mein lieb, mein lieb,* as if its thickening fetal waters could broadcast her longing and reach him, like a shortwave set.

In the dismalest stretches, she wouldn't doze for days. Nor would she admit to Lena the visceral toll of the garment shop—where now, on her own, she needed to spend some full days. Of twenty-five thousand Jews employed on the East Side in 1890, more than twelve thousand were garment workers. By 1899 the growth of the industry, "measured by number of workers and value of product, was two or three times as rapid as the average for all industries." But by 1911 the standard female garment worker nonetheless earned under ten dollars a week.

The shops were ill-lit, poorly ventilated. In some shops a single toilet for up to eighty-five wan workers "passed odors directly into the work space." The gas lighting leaked. The hand-operated pressing irons caused curvature of the spine. Not infrequently, managers hinted for "favors" from the girls. The shop owners often were fellow Jews—that stinks especially, that stinks like a sweatshop toilet late in the shift, in August. By her sixth month, my grandmother couldn't even squeeze behind her machine without a painful intake of breath.

"What *you* do, Lena—is easy?"

"Not so easy, no. They come, these *shloomps,* they don't know if their breath is like a *chazzer's tuchus*" a swine's ass "but their head is filled with the *shtup shtup shtup,* so *nu?*" She shrugged. "So I get filled with the *shtup shtup shtup* a *bissel* mineself. But I tell you, Nettie, I don't got no *troggedik pupik*" pregnant belly-button "and every night with the crying *oy g'vald!* for a bum like this what he leaves you, a tramp he is!"

"Lena . . ."

"A tramp he is, a *shmootz,* say it!"

But the more the censorious Lena inveighed, the less sure my grandmother grew.

Sometimes she'd stop her chopping to listen—some foot on the stair. On certain days she'd think she could hear a hand along the banister. She remembered those hands.

Every day was piecework and onions. Every night, the feather mattress (such luxury!) that she started to wish was a door set hard on two wood crates with his set next to it, touching.

And if then, when she returned to the knife and the vegetable row of work to be done, she didn't hum but under her breath she called the onions *"Tz'drayt-en-kopf! Meshoogeneh!"* like curse words, I can understand. Crazy-in-head! Dummy! Crying, losing track, and dicing the light itself. *"Nar ainer!"* You fool, you! (Him? Herself?) *You-Stupid! My-Fault! Shit-Shit-Shit!* Or more directly—for this was his name—*Albert.*

. . . like a shortwave set . . .

Names, and their powers. Names, and their link to the named.

The names of scalawags, by their occupations, in England in Elizabeth's time: a prigman, a ruffler, a whip-jack, a queerbird, a doxie, a palliard, a tinkard, a kinchin mort, a gyle hather, a nunquam, a dummerer, a demander for glimmer, a bawdy basket, an apple-squire, a scrippet, a nip, a troll hazard of trace. My grandfather, then, was a swigman: "A swigman goeth with a pedlar's pack."

In his study *Jewish Magic and Superstition,* Joshua Trachtenberg says: "The essential character of things and of men resides in their names. Therefore to know a name is to be privy to the secret of its owner's being, and master of his fate. . . . To know the name of a man is to exercise power. One Hebrew text says 'his name is his soul.' "

Even the angels hearkened when they were called. "To set them to work the magician must know the *names* of these angels, for the name was the controlling factor." For instance: "I command you, Haniel, and Hasdiel, and Zadkiel, by these names, to do [thus and thus]," and so were they summoned: Benevolence, Grace, and Mercy.

She'd saved a wisp of hair from his brush, and twisted it into a locket. If she slept at all, she slept clutching this.

Here is how it happened.

Women filled his dreams, his head was a candle-lit bagnio. Sometimes, Nettie's face; sometimes Godiva's. He was embarrassed to wake in front of the other workers, bulging.

Over time, the face was more and more Nettie's. What, what, what to do? "Here." Hi-Step Hank handed over the bottle. "You look like yesterday's bearshit." This was true. This was also, my grandfather knew, an enormous expression of friendship—in terms of its primary roustabout medium, hooch.

So he was drunk that night, approaching Godiva's wagon. Not *too* drunk—voices stopped him. He stood behind a pyramid of water barrels. She'd been drinking too, and Hap the joey.

"Fuck you, mister."

"Fuck you, *sister*. Fuck you and your momma and your momma's momma, with a dry tent pole, and fuck that grunting asshole you make the googoo eyes at."

"You're crazy, you know that? A lard-brain." When she laughed to show disdain, it ran a rich, theatrical scales.

"I ain't blind, we none of us are. You know who."

"The kikey? Oh."

"C'mere." Then there was a minute of urgent breath-sound and nebulous wriggle. When she spoke again, it tumbled quick and emotionally pitched to perfection, as if she'd practiced this set-speech in her own head many times already.

"I like you, Hap. I like to suck you, I like to feel your grubby little fingers spreading my crack. Do you know why?" she didn't wait "All day, I stand in my cherub outfit and twirl on a white horse for the Jesus-drooling citizens of Clean Ass, Kansas, and when they applaud they lift me out of the ring to the Throne of God Himself, and God Himself admires me up on one pink toe and praises my perfection." You could tell, she was posing herself all the while.

"At night I need to get myself filthy, to balance it. You're my filth, Hap. You're my animal stud fucking filth. And on the day I think the kikey man can handle the job" she posed again, to emphasize what *the job* was "he can be my filth too."

"Oh yeah? Well you're—" But he was gone, my grandfather. He didn't need Hap the joey's retort.

Godiva knew something was wrong, when she woke. Through booze-haze she could hear the usual fracas, the bear, the calliope practice . . . something else, though, a terrible wail. She wrapped up in a chenille robe and strode outside. Professor Oink was strung up in back of her wagon, by his aft trotters. He was making one hell of an unacademic squeal. Someone, whoever the lunatic was that did it, had fastened her spangled tutu around him.

But there's another version.

My grandfather woke, so late that even The Great Gambooni was passed out now, making the thrum of a snare drum in his throat.

Come here . . . It was fuzzy outside, and fuzzy inside my grandfather's head. The damn pig seemed to be calling him; that was crazy of course, but after all it was a circus. *Come here* . . . He started in that direction.

Wait . . . Another voice. A dog had gently clipped a loose fold of pajama leg in its teeth. Then it let go, and spoke again. *Come mit me.*

"Who are you?"

I'm a hoont, you can't see? Then: *Who are you?*

"My name is Walter."

Come mit me, Albert. Come, follow mit me.

A foot on the stair. A hand on the banister.

They have too much of anger and healing for us to consider nakedly. I leave them for now on the feather mattress, his first night back. I only want to quote from the *Zohar*, a Jewish mystical text of the *Kabbalah*. It tells us that when a man journeys, his "heavenly wife" is with him all that while—a spirit-form of his matrimonial union remains continuous, and "he is now male and female in the country, as he was male and female in the town." When a man returns from journeying, "it is his duty, once back home, to give his wife pleasure, inasmuch as she it was who obtained for him the heavenly union."

He strokes her taut hill-of-a-belly.

Oi-YOY, mein lieb, mein lieb.

Downstairs, on the table where Mathilde the Queen of the Ocean Deeps once held court, they'd left a loonily-piled Ararat of Hendrickje's underthings. Moonlight through the room's huge windows dappled over it, silver and shadowy blue.

Upstairs, he unfolded himself from the musty cup of her arm. She'd sleep if a meteor hit the garden, now, in the after-exhaustion of sex and a flagon of wine. She always slept well, after reconciliation. He watched her, a moment: here, the moonlight lay like a rosin around her, a malt.

Then he slipped to the studio. There were candles enough. Sleep beckoned him too, but wooing him more imploringly than that was a face from his sketchbook. With the canvas sized from last week, he could start it into oils tonight, while the burning was on him. A Jewess's face—it had broken out of a small complacence of faces by the tumult of emotions it wore. And this excited him, thinking the paint would soon be human skin, and then the skin would be that mixspot where a woman's acquiescence meets her hard determination, now a tittle of indigo, gray, red, thickly squiggled salmon . . . particularizing the chisel-edge of light along her nape and then into the tassels of hair below one ear, and over the jaw set slightly off center in thought . . .

Preserving this one face—doleful, triumphant, whatever—as best he can, and while he can, while it still isn't doused from his system.

She turned. The half-moon lit her face and would have made it timelessly lovely, except an upright from the fire escape flung one long bar of shadow across her.

"I think we will call him the name of Ervin."

"Yes, a good name." He sighed, immensely. "Such a day, Nettie . . ."

"Such a life."

"Yes." Then he paused, he was ashamed. "With this *kaddishel*" this baby boy "he'll be here soon . . ."

"Or a girl, yah. Then Hannah we call her."

"... but the money, I don't have this. From a circus, they don't give the money so much. A place to be, peoples you talk with, yes; but the money, no. So . . ." he halted, he'd never failed this way.

She opened her second-hand steamer trunk and withdrew the celluloid whatnot box. Twelve dollars a week, six months—it was a fortune, 288 dollars.

"Nettie! How do you make this for us, from nothing?"

"*Kishef,*" she told him—magic.

"It isn't always a happy ending, is it?" Gaylene has exhibited, for my histrionic oohing, every porcelain nixie, 1920s bakelite bangle, and near-mint first-edition Oz series title in her apartment. We've even played with the Schoenhut figurines, doing seal noise (ROWK! ROWK!), tiger-and-lion growl, crowd hubbahubba. But what we can't do is conjure Craig, and what *I* can't do is love her enough in the way I do love her to make that not matter.

Later, I visit Craig. He's getting along, he says. We knock back some beers on the building's crumbling balcony, then a few more beers. He isn't getting along, he says then. What went wrong? Didn't they *try* hard?

It's a rhetorical question; no one tried harder. We sit there in silence, surrounded by the kit-kat clocks with moving eyes, the toby mugs, the inkwells and quills, the frog and ostrich and bulldog and Martian and porcupine rubber squeeze-me toys, the turn-of-the-century printer's type, the cowboy lamps, the vastly tasteless selection of lime-green naugahyde.

They'd saved everything imaginable *except* Hitler's brain—and their marriage.

᛭

7. Postscript: *The Final Entry*

I was still in Oklahoma when I exited: some dried-out, moon-cratered place. Its squalid version of an oasis was a makeshift dump where broken box-spring mattresses and shattered toilets, unsavable and long past any compromise with use or sensibility, wavered like bad TV reception, in the upshaft heat of decay. I pulled alongside it, into its swimming stink. Austin was science-fiction distance south of me; Wichita, north.

This wasn't the plan, of course. I couldn't have done it, *planned*. But I unloaded the trunk, the back seat, and the U-Haul minihitch with a swift efficiency that normally only preparedness could account for. Thirty cartons of lousy job and soured marriage, with the scarab-green and iridescent blackberry sheen of compost flies already in exploratory orbits.

I could have flown the Dodge Colt home, it felt so light.

You need to know when to let go. Otherwise . . .

Jeanmarie, a friend, has a story. Her grandmother's died and the family holds a traditional nightlong keening and tippling Catholic/Irish wake. Everyone slobbering piteously, getting juiced, emitting great shaken-out moans from the heartcore, throwing themselves across the open coffin as if with suttee in mind, and in general wreaking very grievous and merry prefunereal havoc.

"Some time before sunup my grandfather lifted her corpse from the coffin and started dancing, *ballroom dancing,* around the room. They couldn't pry him away from her, maybe they half didn't want to. He couldn't let go of her. Dancing. His hand at the small of her back." Dancing around the room until the candles burned down as flat as wax coins.

In 1656 the court ordered Rembrandt's holdings cataloged for sale. He was deeply in debt, and this euphemistic *cessio bonorum,* a "surrender of goods," replaced the harsher official declaration of bankruptcy saved for the truly fraudulent. Everything went— the gold helmets, the walrus-tusk carvings, everything. The inventory taker from the Chamber of Insolvent Estates compiled 363 separate entries.

Kenneth Clark says, "It is usually supposed that the sale of all these precious possessions was a great blow to him. But who can tell?" (Mee seconds this uncertainty: "There is no way to know how Rembrandt was feeling during all this.") Then Clark philosophizes, "There is a point at which possessions become a burden: they are exhilarating to buy, but a nuisance to look after. What if moths had got into the fur caps, and the Japanese armour had rusted, and pupils had spilt turpentine on his Marcantonio engravings and poisoned his pet monkey (which one of them actually did). The grandest and calmest of all his self-portraits was done in the year of his sale."

He's ruminating out of the frame—but inwardly, at the same time—with a kind of understanding resignation, and this somehow doesn't negate, but deepens, poignantizes, the natural big-bodied majesty.

In Lewis Hyde's insightful study *The Gift,* he tells us, "A gift is a thing we do not get by our own efforts. We cannot buy it; we cannot acquire it through an act of will. It is bestowed upon us." In a sense, my finding *Green Lantern* No. 3 is such a gift, hoped for but unarrangeable, surely a moment of grace in which the cosmos let me open up Time and take a step retrograde into it; and the thirty dollars is not so much the price of a commodity, as the necessary clearing away of a space where serendipity occurs. No matter what a comics price guide says, there is no market value for such an occasion; it exists in its own green atemporal shimmer.

Hyde continues, "Thus we rightly speak of 'talent' as a 'gift,' for although a talent can be perfected through an effort of the will, no effort in the world can cause its initial appearance. Mozart, composing on the harpsichord at the age of four, had a gift." And Rembrandt stretches his arm on the table, rests his head in its bend, and sighs his way at last into a fitful slumber, under the half-complete painting. This is where we take our leave of him.

"Moreover, a gift that cannot be given away ceases to be a gift.

The spirit of a gift is kept alive by its constant donation. May Sarton writes: 'The gift turned inward, unable to be given, becomes a heavy burden, even sometimes a kind of poison. It is as though the flow of life were backed up.' It is the talent which is not in use that is lost or atrophies, and to bestow one of our creations is the surest way to invoke the next. Bestowal creates that empty place into which new energy may flow. The alternative is petrifaction, writer's block, 'the flow of life backed up.'"

For any ongoing, then, there needs to be an equal emptying out: the tile mosaic must leave the artist's studio for the gallery; the lover must carry his knit wool keepsake into battle; the High Gods must look down with a gaze that meets the burnt offering wafting up on a chargray plume of sacrifice smoke.

This is one of the ancientmost wars: a page of Yiddish, fixing the years and their passions against disappearance; and the man with the match, who needs to get on with the thousand-and-one tugs of living.

This is the final entry in Nathaniel Hawthorne's *American Notebooks:* "I burned great heaps of old letters, and other papers, a little while ago, preparatory to going to England. Among them were hundreds of ———'s letters. The world has no more such, and now they are all dust and ashes. What a trustful guardian of secret matters is fire! What should we do without fire and death?"

AFTERWORD

These essays were written over ten years, not always with my eye on their being gathered together: each had its separate beckon. Still, I've tried in retrospect to fashion them into a meaningful community. In doing so, I've come to forgive the little inconsistencies, and to find a functional, resonant motif in the little repetitions that result from these essays' now being collected into one large unit. I'll trust you have similar empathy.

The research material I've gratefully relied upon is often credited within the text of the essays themselves. Every reasonable effort to credit sources has been made, but ten years is a long time in this unorganized, well-intentioned but haphazard record-keeper's life; and I ask understanding for any omissions that have slipped through my mounded ziggurats of scrap paper notes. The following sources were acknowledged, with deep appreciation, when these essays originally appeared in literary journals:

Eadward Muybridge: The Man Who Invented the Moving Picture (MacDonnell); *Phenomena: A Book of Wonders* (Mitchell and Rickard); *Prairie Fires and Paper Moons* (Morgan and Brown); *Mary Shelley's Monster* (Tropp); *The Birth of the Modern* (Johnson); *The Nascent Mind of Shelley* (Hughes); *A Newton Among Poets* (Grabo); *Weird Ways to Die* (Doyle); *Elsa Lanchester Remembered* (Ackerman); *Poets and Their Art* (Monroe); *Midwest Portraits* (Hansen); *Poems and Psalms* (Carroll); *The Story of the Armory Show* (Brown); *Edgar Rice Burroughs,*

Master of Adventure (Lupoff); *Edgar Rice Burroughs, the Man Who Created Tarzan* (Porges); *The Evolution of Useless Things* (Petroski); *Picasso, Creator and Destroyer* (Huffington); *High and Low* (Varnedoe and Gopnik); *New York 1913* (Green); *Owning It All* (Kittredge); "On Collecting" (Perl); *Rembrandt's Portrait* (Mee); *World of Our Fathers* (Howe); *Habitations of the Word* (Gass); *A Sense of the Future* (Bronowski); "Preserving the Printed Word" (Benjamin); *Jewish Magic and Superstition* (Trachtenberg); *An Introduction to Rembrandt* (Clark); *The Gift* (Hyde); and poems by Louis Simpson and Kenneth Koch.

> *Oyf a masse fegt men nit keyn kashke.*
> Don't ask questions—it's a story.
>   —Yiddish proverb

Albert Goldbarth lives in Wichita, Kansas. He is the author of two earlier collections of essays. Also, for a quarter of a century he has been publishing notable books of poetry, including *Heaven and Earth: A Cosmology* (recipient of the National Book Critics Circle Award) and *Across the Layers: Poems Old and New,* both published by the University of Georgia Press.